Dear Friends,

It's hard to imagine what it is like living without pizza, pancakes or a tasty sandwich for lunch. But for the millions who cannot eat foods with gluten—the protein found in wheat, barley, rye and some oats—it's a challenge they face every day.

Knowing there's a need for tasty recipes made with gluten-free ingredients, such as Betty Crocker® Gluten Free Cake Mixes, Bisquick® mix or Chex® cereal, we contacted **Silvana Nardone**, (see foreword on page 4) author of *Cooking for Isaiah: Gluten-Free & Dairy-Free Recipes for Easy, Delicious Meals* and **Jean Duane**, author of *Bake Deliciously! Gluten and Dairy Free Cookbook*. They teamed up with the Betty Crocker® Kitchens to develop recipes for those who need to (or choose to) follow a gluten-free diet.

The best part is these recipes are delicious for the whole family. We triple-tested all of them in the Betty Crocker® Kitchens to make sure you can easily make them at home. Enjoy family favorites like banana bread, dinner rolls, even homemade pizza and amazing desserts. Check out our guide to Safe to Consume Gluten-Free Ingredients and Easy to Overlook Sources of Gluten plus Tips for Working with Gluten-Free Ingredients. Also, visit GlutenFreely.com for a list of more than 300 gluten-free products, hear from our bloggers, sign up for our free monthly newsletter, and save on over 400 delicious gluten-free foods that can be shipped right to your door, many of which are found in these recipes! Our mission is simple: To help you live a delicious life, gluten freely.

Warmly,
Betty Crocker

FOREWORD

It's a brand new gluten-free world out there—a reality that could only be achieved by committing to improve the texture and flavor of every single gluten-free meal and dessert that comes out of our kitchens.

I'm happy to be part of this transformation, along with my friends at Betty Crocker and fellow cookbook author, Jean Duane. Together, we have dedicated ourselves to recreating all of our family's favorite foods—one recipe at a time.

In *Betty Crocker Gluten-Free Cooking,* we share our personal cooking and baking secrets, so you can live your life as you've always imagined—with a table overflowing with satisfying food the whole family can enjoy. Imagine eating fluffy pancakes, crusty pizza and flaky pie again—no worry, no guilt. They're all here in this cookbook.

Now, more than ever before, everything you've hoped for is within your reach.

Love,
Silvana Nardone

Author of *Cooking for Isaiah:*
Gluten-Free & Dairy-Free
Recipes for Easy, Delicious Meals

Contents

quick ready to eat in 30 minutes or less

easy prep time of 15 minutes or less

lowfat main dishes with 10g of fat or less, all other 3g of fat or less

What Is Gluten?

Gluten is a protein naturally found in certain grains such as wheat, barley, rye and some oats. Consequently any foods that are made with these grains also contain gluten—that includes foods such as bagels, breads, cakes, cereals, cookies, crackers, pasta, pizza and more.

Who Should Avoid Gluten?

About three million Americans suffer from an inherited autoimmune disorder called celiac disease (or celiac sprue). The disease affects the digestive process of the small intestine and is triggered by the consumption of gluten.

If you are affected by celiac disease, eating gluten or gluten-containing foods triggers an autoimmune reaction that leads to inflammation and damage to the lining of the small intestine called the mucosa (where foods go after they have been eaten and digested). This damage makes it very difficult for your body to absorb nutrients from the foods you eat. Over time, a damaged small intestine can lead to malnourishment and other possible complications such as loss of bone density, iron deficiency anemia, villous atrophy (flattening of the finger-like villi that stick out from the mucosa and help with absorption), gastrointestinal and neurological symptoms and quality of life issues. If you have celiac disease, the only treatment is to follow a gluten-free diet—that is, to avoid all foods containing gluten. For most people, following this diet will heal existing intestinal damage and prevent further damage.

How to Know If It's Celiac Disease?

Celiac disease affects people differently. There are hundreds of signs and symptoms of celiac disease, yet many people with celiac disease have no symptoms at all. Symptoms of celiac disease are varied. For example, you might have diarrhea and abdominal pain, while someone else might develop infertility or anemia. Children tend to have more classic signs of celiac disease, including growth problems (failure to thrive), gastrointestinal issues (constipation/diarrhea, abdominal pain), fatigue and irritability. Adults tend to have a variety of symptoms—only some of which may be gastrointestinal—making celiac disease often difficult to diagnose. Celiac disease runs in families. That means if you have celiac disease, your children and siblings are at higher risk for having the disease and must be tested for the condition.

Screening for celiac disease can be done through both genetic and antibody tests. The genetic test tells if you have the genes that lead to the development of celiac disease. This test is also good to rule out the disease. The antibody blood test will show if your body is responding in a negative way to gluten. A positive result for either type of test requires follow-up for a diagnosis. An endoscopic biopsy (a tissue sample taken from the small intestine villi) is necessary to confirm the diagnosis of celiac disease.

What Is Gluten Sensitivity?

Gluten may also be avoided by those who are sensitive to it, or make a personal choice to avoid it. Non-celiac gluten sensitivity is the name used to describe someone who tests negative for celiac disease, but whose symptoms subside when they eliminate gluten from their diet. Scientific evidence supports that gluten sensitivity not only exists—but is quite different from celiac disease.

Science shows that the immune reaction to gluten sensitivity is indeed different from the immune reaction to celiac disease, though some of the symptoms may be similar. There are no definitive tests to determine if you or someone in your family has non-celiac gluten sensitivity—but experts recommend that if you think you are sensitive to gluten, you should be tested for celiac disease first. For now, eating a gluten-free diet is the only treatment recommended for gluten sensitivity.

Nutritional Considerations with Celiac Disease

Celiac disease presents a number of nutritional concerns for those affected by it. If you have celiac disease and you consume gluten, your immune system responds by attacking the small intestine and inhibiting the absorption of important nutrients into the body.

Following a gluten-free diet long term can improve a variety of outcomes related to bone density, iron deficiency anemia and more. However, managing celiac disease is not just about eliminating gluten from your diet. If you are affected with celiac disease, you must take extra care to ensure that you get all the vitamins and nutrients you need—particularly calcium, iron, fiber, whole grains and B vitamins. In many cases, a gluten-free vitamin and mineral supplement may be recommended to provide extra assurance that nutrition needs are being met. If you or your child has celiac disease, a doctor, dietitian or healthcare provider can help determine what is right for you or your family.

Calcium & Vitamin D

Calcium is an essential mineral for bone growth and development—and it may not be absorbed properly in people with celiac disease. Poor calcium absorption can cause abnormal bone growth, a greater risk of broken bones, as well as painful bones and joints. Scientific research trials and cross-sectional studies have shown reduced bone mineral content and reduced bone mineral density (osteopenia/osteoporosis) in untreated adults with celiac disease. Since vitamin D helps with calcium absorption, it is important for you to include gluten-free foods that are rich in calcium and vitamin D.

Iron

Iron is an essential mineral necessary for many important functions in the body. It is part of hemoglobin—the oxygen-carrying component of the blood. Not getting enough iron can lead to anemia, which can cause severe weakness and fatigue. If you have iron-deficiency anemia and celiac disease, eating foods rich in iron such as lean red meats and fortified breakfast cereals—in addition to taking a daily gluten-free multivitamin supplement with iron—may be recommended.

Whole Grains and Fiber

Nine out of ten Americans don't eat enough whole grains or fiber. And even though the availability and variety of gluten-free items is increasing, finding whole grain and fiber-rich gluten-free foods can be challenging. The 2010 Dietary Guidelines for Americans recommend eating half of all grains as whole grains and eating more fiber-containing legumes, vegetables, fruits and whole grains as well.

"Whole grain" means the complete grain kernel—bran, germ, endosperm. Eating three servings or more of foods made with whole grain each day as part of a healthy diet may help protect heart health, manage weight and reduce risk for certain types of cancer and diabetes. If you are affected by celiac disease, you can easily add gluten-free whole grains such as brown rice, popcorn, quinoa (pronounced "keen wah"), buckwheat (which does not contain wheat), amaranth and other gluten-free whole grain products to help get the three servings of whole grains recommended daily.

Fiber helps with digestion, laxation and a feeling of fullness. People who eat more fiber tend to have healthier body weights; soluble fiber from oats and fruits contributes to heart health—and can help lower cholesterol when eaten as part of a heart healthy diet. There are many gluten-free grains that are excellent sources of fiber. Some examples include: buckwheat, flaxseed, quinoa and amaranth. Beans (dry beans/legumes), nuts, fruits and vegetables are also great foods to include to help meet the 25 to 35 grams of fiber recommended daily for adults.

B vitamins

The changes to the small intestine make it difficult to absorb nutrients such as B vitamins, causing some level of deficiency to occur. B vitamins act as part of co-enzymes—complexes that help support a number of different functions in the body such as metabolism. Thiamin, riboflavin and niacin typically added to enriched grains may be missing from gluten-free diets—as these grains are eliminated. Supplementing with pyridoxine (vitamin B_6), vitamin B_{12} and folic acid (vitamin B_9) have shown to improve deficiencies in celiac disease patients in recent studies. Check with your healthcare team to determine what is right for you or your child.

Healthful Gluten-Free Eating

Many foods are naturally free of gluten, unless it was added during manufacturing or through cross contamination in your own kitchen. If you follow a gluten-free diet, you can enjoy a variety of foods including:

Beans and legumes
Corn
Eggs
Flax
Fresh beef, lamb and pork
Fresh chicken and turkey
Fresh fish and shellfish
Fruits
Lentils
Milk
Nuts and seeds
Potatoes
Quinoa
Rice and wild rice
Soy
Vegetables

Easy-to-Overlook Sources of Gluten

Some foods may contain gluten even though they don't seem like they might. Some frequently overlooked foods or ingredients that may be sources of hidden gluten include:

Barbecue sauce
Broth
Candy
Coating mixes
Croutons
Flavorings
Gravies
Imitation bacon
Imitation seafood (surimi)
Marinades
Medications and supplements that contain binders
Panko (Japanese-style bread crumbs)
Play-Doh®
Processed meats
Rotisserie chicken
Salad dressings
Sauces
Sauce mixes
Seasonings
Soups
Soy sauce
Sweet and sour sauce
Teriyaki sauce
Thickeners
Vegetarian meat substitutes
Wheat starch

Success Tips for Working with Gluten-Free Ingredients

As you adapt to living gluten freely, try some of these tips to make your efforts a success.

- Keep a variety of gluten-free ingredients on hand—Most recipes require several ingredients to replace wheat flour so you'll want to be prepared.

- Store ingredients in zip-seal bags—Packages open to the air will spoil more quickly. Using airtight zip-seal bags will help keep ingredients fresher.

- Use the fridge or freezer to prolong shelf life—Since grains contain fat that can become rancid easily at room temperature, you'll want to retain the freshness of your ingredients by storing them in the fridge or freezer.

- Line up your ingredients when baking—Create an assembly line of ingredients in the same order as the recipe so you don't forget anything. As you use each one, move it off to the side.

- Experiment with various gluten-free flours, gums and starches—Each gluten-free ingredient has unique properties. Trying different combinations of ingredients can provide successful baking outcomes.

- Expect some trial and error when reconfiguring recipes—Gluten-free baking requires patience. Sometimes the recipe changes you make may not work out exactly as expected.

Creating a Gluten-Free Kitchen

Knowing which foods are naturally gluten free, plus knowing what to look for when reading labels are keys to getting started with a gluten-free lifestyle. Eating and cooking gluten free means making a number of other changes too. Simple things that you and your family didn't think about before will need to be addressed. Learning how to keep a gluten-free kitchen will take time to assure that mistakes aren't made and gluten-free eaters stay healthy. Learning where to buy gluten-free foods, for example, may mean making a separate trip to another store or purchasing some gluten-free products online.

Establishing Practices for Living Gluten Freely

When you're getting started living a gluten-free lifestyle, it's important to take steps to keep things free from contact with gluten—also called cross contamination. This is especially true when everyone in the household is not eating gluten free. Be sure to communicate with all family members exactly how you plan to keep the kitchen free from gluten. Consider these ideas for maintaining a gluten-free kitchen:

- **Be Clean.** Wash everything well in very hot, soapy water. That means your hands, countertops, utensils, knives, spoon rests, bowls, cutting boards, measuring cups and spoons, pots, pans and colanders. Even a small amount of stuck-on pasta or a few crumbs can contain enough gluten to make you feel sick. You may even want to have a gluten-free sponge and hand towel too.

- **Try Color Coding.** Have a separate gluten-free cutting board that is easy to identify—such as a different color. That way the usual (gluten-contaminated) cutting board can be used by most family members—keeping a gluten-free board of another color separate and free from gluten.

- **Use Separate Utensils.** A spoon used with gluten-containing foods cannot be used with gluten-free foods unless it is washed thoroughly between uses.

Be conscientious or purchase a separate set of cooking utensils. If color coding works well as a visual reminder, choose a handle color to match your gluten-free cutting board or gluten-free sponge and towel.

- **Label Spaces.** Designate a specific shelf or cabinet as gluten free. Clean it thoroughly first and label it prominently to be sure family members honor the gluten-free code. Choose an upper shelf so gluten particles don't fall onto it by accident. This works for the fridge and freezer too.

- **Use Toaster Etiquette.** If washing off the toaster racks after each use is difficult to maintain, use aluminum foil in the toaster to protect gluten-free foods from contamination or designate a tray that is gluten-free so gluten-free foods don't touch surfaces that contain crumbs from gluten. Alternatively, if you have plenty of counter space, you can choose to have a separate gluten-free toaster.

- **Get the Squeeze.** Only use clean knives and spoons in condiments, jellies and jams, with no double dipping. If that proves difficult or if you have young children in the house, opt for squeeze versions of condiments being careful that the tip doesn't touch any food (and wiping it off, if it does).

- **Fry Gluten-Free.** Oil used to fry foods containing gluten should not be used for gluten-free items. Keep a separate fryer or fry gluten-free foods first, then fry gluten-containing foods and discard the oil so mistakes are avoided.

Buying Gluten-Free Foods

Making a switch to gluten-free eating is easier today than in years past. To eat gluten freely means purchasing a range and variety of ingredients—many of which may be new to you. Gluten-free recipes often call for several ingredients to replace wheat flour. Try the recipes for homemade Gluten-Free All-Purpose Flour Blend or Gluten-Free Quick Bread Mix provided on page 15 or experiment with creating your own gluten-free flour blends. Read the purchasing information below that can help you know where to shop:

- **Produce section.** Shop the bounty of fresh fruits and vegetables at your grocery store or visit a local farmer's market. These naturally gluten-free favorites offer nutrients, fiber and more. Frozen and canned items can fit too—but be sure to read the labels and purchase foods plain without sauces and coatings.

- **Fresh meats, poultry, fish and shellfish.** Check out the meat and fish sections of your grocery store, or visit a local butcher or seafood vendor. These foods are naturally free of gluten and provide protein and many of the nutrients you and your family need to stay healthy. Again, avoid items that are fried, coated or already prepared in sauces or broths that may contain hidden sources of gluten.

- **Grains and flours.** The number of gluten-free flours, pastas and grains in grocery stores is growing. Seek out whole grain varieties and those that are enriched to take advantage of the vitamins, minerals and fiber they contain. Look for quinoa, amaranth, brown rice, millet, sorghum, buckwheat, cornmeal, tapioca flour, rice flour, black bean flour, fava bean flour and rice noodles.

- **Ethnic aisle.** With traditional grocery stores expanding their offerings, it's easy to find many gluten-free items in the Asian section, ethnic aisle or natural section of the store. Comb the shelves for xanthan gum, arrowroot, cornstarch, potato starch flour, kasha (buckwheat groats), rice noodles and gluten-free soy sauce.

- **Food co-ops.** Food co-ops often carry a big variety of grains—many of which are gluten free. They sometimes have a gluten-free section too that makes it easy for you to purchase special ingredients. Because sanitary practices can vary and are hard to monitor, it's best to skip the bulk bins and dispensers. Look for pre-packaged cornmeal, amaranth, quinoa ("keen wah"), sorghum, millet, rice varieties, brown rice flour, fava bean flour and almond meal.

- **Specialty stores.** Asian markets and specialty stores are other places to find gluten-free ingredients. Check sell-by dates to be sure you are purchasing fresh foods. Rice paper wrappers, rice noodles, white rice flour, and soba (buckwheat) noodles and other products can be found here.

- **Online and mail-order outlets.** If you live in a small town or rural area with stores that don't stock many gluten-free ingredients, look online or try mail order. Websites such as www.glutenfreely.com, www.bobsredmill.com/gluten-free/ and www.amazon.com/glutenfree carry gluten-free ingredients and products that you can buy to try or purchase in bulk. Find out the return policy before you order, and be certain you have enough gluten-free space for storage.

- **Name-brand gluten-free options.** Certain brands only exist as gluten-free foods—and they may be brands you never heard of. Yet there are many name-brand products such as Betty Crocker® Gluten Free cake, brownie and cookie mixes, Bisquick® Gluten Free mix, and Chex® cereals that are manufactured gluten free. These convenient foods can make it easier to adjust to a gluten-free lifestyle.

Reading Labels to Avoid Gluten

The best way to know if a product is gluten free is to read the ingredients label. To determine if a product contains gluten, there are four main words to know: wheat, barley, rye and oats. Also look for ingredients that are derived from these grains.

Looking for any of these four words will help identify products that contain gluten. Check product labels on every shopping trip. It's the best way to identify what a food or beverage contains. And since ingredients and products can change over time, monitor ingredient labels regularly to know which foods are gluten free. Even if a product does not contain these obvious sources of gluten, you may wish to contact the product manufacturer to confirm gluten-free status. Below is a more detailed list of ingredients to avoid as they contain wheat, barley, rye, oats, or derivatives of these grains:

Abyssinian hard (Wheat *Triticum durum*)	Croutons
Avena (wild oat)	Dinkel*
Barley (*Hordeum vulgare*)	Durum*
Barley malt, barley extract	Edible starch
Beer, ale, porter, stout, other fermented beverages	Einkorn, wild einkorn*
	Emmer, wild emmer*
Blue cheese**	Farina
Bran	Farro*
Bread, bread flour, breading, coating	Filler
Bouillon	Flour (including, but not limited to: all-purpose, barley, bleached, bread, brown, durum, enriched, gluten, graham, granary, high protein, high gluten, oat, wheat, white)
Bulgur (bulgur wheat, bulgur nuts)	
Cereal (cereal extract, cereal binding)	
Chapatti flour (atta)	
Couscous	Fu
Cracker meal	Germ

Gluten, glutenin	Rice malt, rice syrup, brown rice syrup**
Graham flour	Rye
Hordeum (*Hordeum vulgare*)	Seitan
Hydrolyzed oat starch, hydrolyzed wheat gluten, hydrolyzed wheat protein	Semolina
Kamut*	Soy Sauce**
Malt, malt beverages, malt extract, malted milk, malt flavoring, malt syrup, malt vinegar	Spelt*
	Sprouted wheat
Matzo, Matzah (meal, farfel, flour)	Stuffing
MIR (wheat, rye)	Tabbouleh
Miso (may contain barley)	Triticale
Mustard powder**	Udon
Oats†, oat bran, oat fiber, oat gum, oat syrup	Vital gluten
Oriental wheat	Wheat, wheat berry, wheat bran, wheat germ, wheat germ oil, wheat grass, wheat gluten, wheat starch, whole wheat berries
Orzo	

*Types of wheat.
**May be made with wheat.
†Historically, oats were not recommended because it was thought that avenin (the storage protein found in oats) was also toxic to gluten-intolerant individuals. However, recent research in Europe and the U.S. has described that oats are well tolerated by most children and adults when consumed in moderation and do not contribute to abdominal symptoms, nor prevent intestinal healing. PLEASE NOTE: regular, commercially available oats are frequently cross contaminated with wheat or barley during harvesting, milling or processing. However, "pure, uncontaminated" oats have recently become available from several companies in the U.S. and Canada. These companies process oats in dedicated facilities and their oats are tested for purity. Pure, uncontaminated oats can be consumed safely in quantities < 1 cup per day. It is important that you talk to your physician and your registered dietitian prior to starting oats.

Dining Out Gluten-Free

Dining out when you have special dietary needs can be stressful. Even if you're careful, simple mistakes in the kitchen can mean gluten contamination and getting sick. It's all in the planning! Here's how to plan to stay gluten free—even if the restaurant isn't.

FIND CELIAC-FRIENDLY VENUES. With the increasing awareness of celiac disease and gluten-free living, more and more restaurants are catering to customers who must avoid gluten. Check out websites such as www.glutenfreerestaurants.org and www.glutenfreeregistry.com for restaurants in your area and in locations where you plan to travel.

PREVIEW MENUS. Many restaurants post their menus online so you can know what to expect even before making a reservation. If you're already on-the-go, download gluten-free menu applications for your mobile device so you can easily browse gluten-free restaurant offerings. Visit http://glutenfreepassport.com.

PHONE AHEAD. Call the restaurant in late afternoon when it isn't busy. Speak to the chef or kitchen manager who will be in charge on the day you plan to visit to make sure they can meet your gluten-free needs. If you feel at all uncomfortable or unsure about the discussion, you can opt to dine elsewhere.

ARRIVE AT QUIET TIMES. Schedule your visit at slightly off-peak times. Your server will have more time to answer questions, and the kitchen will be better able to handle special requests when it's less busy. Check in with the manager when you arrive to be sure they understand your gluten-free needs. Plan for extra time as it may take the kitchen longer to prepare your special meal.

PRACTICE WHAT TO SAY. It's also a good idea to rehearse your explanation about having celiac disease. Consider saying that you're on a special diet and you can become very sick from eating wheat, oats, bread, flour, croutons or soy sauce, for example. Explain that even if your food touches those foods, it can make you sick too.

PRESENT A CARD. A simple wallet-size card listing what you can and cannot eat will educate the kitchen and servers. Having the card in several languages can be helpful if you live in an area where multiple languages are spoken. Create a separate card for travel in the language(s) of your destination. Check out www.triumphdining.com for dining cards and other useful tools and resources for eating out.

ASK QUESTIONS. Being your own advocate is the best way to assure you stay gluten free. Pose questions to the servers if anything isn't clear. Ask about croutons on the salad or soy sauce in the marinade. Your best bet may be ordering plain foods without sauce, stuffing or coatings. Have a second option ready in case your first choice can't be prepared gluten freely.

BE A REGULAR. If you find a restaurant that accommodates your needs and where you enjoy the food, visit often. They'll get to know you, and your needs will be met more readily. If you find a server who really understands your needs or goes out of their way to accommodate you, tip them well and be sure to request them the next time you visit.

Finding a Favorite Gluten-Free Flour Blend

One way to achieve success with baking gluten freely is to find or create a homemade gluten-free flour blend or two that works well for your baking needs. One advantage is that you can mix up the flour blend ahead of time and store it in the freezer. That way it's ready for you, when you plan to bake—cutting down on preparation time.

The work is done for you with this Gluten-Free All-Purpose Flour Blend recipe for cakes, coffee cakes and more. It is used in the recipes for Boston Cream Pie (page 197), Cinnamon Roll Pound Cake with Vanilla Drizzle (page 198) and Hazelnut Streusel Coffee Cake (page 55). You can also try the recipe for Gluten-Free Quick Bread Mix that can be used in recipes for Applesauce Quick Bread (page 132), Cinnamon Raisin Bread (page 131) and Gingerbread Molasses Flax Muffins (page 133) as well as to modify your own muffin, scone and quick bread recipes.

Gluten-Free All-Purpose Flour Blend

Prep Time: 5 Minutes • Start to Finish: 5 Minutes • 4 pounds (13 cups)

3¾ cups brown rice flour

3¾ cups white rice flour

3¾ cups tapioca flour

1¾ cups plus 2 tablespoons potato starch flour

2 tablespoons plus 1½ teaspoons xanthan gum

3¾ teaspoons salt

1 In large bowl, mix all ingredients with whisk until fully incorporated. Transfer to storage container; seal tightly. Store in cool, dry place or in refrigerator. Before using, stir to blend the flours and xanthan gum.

Contributed by Silvana Nardone Silvana's Kitchen http://silvanaskitchen.com

Gluten-Free Quick Bread Mix

Prep Time: 10 Minutes • Start to Finish: 10 Minutes • 6½ cups

1½ cups white rice flour

1½ cups tapioca flour

¾ cup potato starch flour

¾ cup sweet white sorghum flour

¾ cup garbanzo and fava flour

¾ cup cornstarch

3 teaspoons xanthan gum

3 teaspoons gluten-free baking powder

3 teaspoons baking soda

1½ teaspoons salt

1 In large bowl, mix all ingredients with whisk until fully incorporated. Spoon into large resealable freezer plastic bag. Store in freezer 6 to 9 months. Before using, shake bag thoroughly for several minutes to blend the flours and xanthan gum.

Contributed by Jean Duane Alternative Cook http://www.alternativecook.com

appetizers & snacks

Cheesy Herb and Beef Bites

Prep Time: 15 Minutes • Start to Finish: 15 Minutes • 40 appetizers

10 thin slices gluten-free deli roast beef, about 4 inches in diameter (from 6-oz package)

¼ cup garlic-and-herbs spreadable cheese (from 4- to 6.5-oz container)

¼ cup finely chopped red bell pepper

2 unpeeled cucumbers, cut into 40 slices

1 Unfold each beef slice so that it is flat. Spread each slice with 1 teaspoon cheese and 1 teaspoon bell pepper. Carefully roll up.

2 Cut each roll into 4 pieces. Place each beef roll on cucumber slice. Serve immediately.

1 Appetizer: Calories 15 (Calories from Fat 10); Total Fat 1g (Saturated Fat 0g; Trans Fat 0g); Cholesterol 0mg; Sodium 5mg; Total Carbohydrate 0g (Dietary Fiber 0g); Protein 0g **% Daily Value:** Vitamin A 0%; Vitamin C 4%; Calcium 0%; Iron 0% **Exchanges:** Free **Carbohydrate Choices:** 0

Get a jump start on preparing these bites— follow step 1, then cover and refrigerate rolls up to 8 hours. Cut each roll into 4 pieces, and continue as directed.

Turkey slices can be substituted for the roast beef.

Pastrami and Pepper Roll-Ups

Prep Time: 25 Minutes • Start to Finish: 2 Hours 25 Minutes • 40 appetizers

½ lb thinly sliced gluten-free pastrami (from deli)

⅓ cup chives-and-onion cream cheese spread (from 8-oz container)

½ cup roasted red bell peppers (from 12-oz jar), drained, cut into ¾-inch-wide strips

Fresh rosemary sprigs, if desired

1 Spread each pastrami slice with cream cheese spread. Top each with roasted pepper piece at one edge. Starting at roasted pepper edge, roll up each tightly. Cover; refrigerate at least 2 hours or until firm.

2 To serve, cut each roll into 1-inch-thick pieces. Secure each with fresh rosemary sprig or cocktail toothpick.

1 Appetizer: Calories 15 (Calories from Fat 10); Total Fat 1g (Saturated Fat 0.5g; Trans Fat 0g); Cholesterol 0mg; Sodium 90mg; Total Carbohydrate 0g (Dietary Fiber 0g); Protein 1g **% Daily Value:** Vitamin A 2%; Vitamin C 4%; Calcium 0%; Iron 0% **Exchanges:** Free **Carbohydrate Choices:** 0

Always read labels to make sure each recipe ingredient is gluten-free. Products and ingredient sources can change.

Basil and Roasted Red Pepper Bites

Prep Time: 25 Minutes • Start to Finish: 2 Hours 25 Minutes • 25 appetizers

1 package (2.5 oz) thinly sliced gluten-free deli ham

3 tablespoons reduced-fat garden vegetable cream cheese spread (from 8-oz container)

1 package (⅔ oz) fresh basil leaves

⅓ cup roasted red bell peppers (from 12-oz jar), patted dry

5 pieces (5½ inches long) string cheese

1 Stack 2 slices ham on work surface; pat dry with paper towel. Spread evenly with 1½ to 2 teaspoons cream cheese. Top with basil leaves to within 1 inch of top edge. Cut roasted peppers into 1-inch strips; cut to fit width of ham. Place pepper strips across bottom edge of ham. Place cheese piece above pepper on basil leaves; trim to fit.

2 Beginning at bottom edge, roll up securely. Wrap in plastic wrap. Repeat with remaining ingredients to make 5 rolls. Refrigerate 2 hours.

3 Unwrap rolls; place seam sides down. With sharp serrated knife, cut each roll into 5 pieces. If desired, pierce each roll with 5 evenly spaced toothpicks before cutting.

1 Appetizer: Calories 45 (Calories from Fat 25); Total Fat 3g (Saturated Fat 1.5g; Trans Fat 0g); Cholesterol 10mg; Sodium 90mg; Total Carbohydrate 0g (Dietary Fiber 0g); Protein 4g **% Daily Value:** Vitamin A 4%; Vitamin C 2%; Calcium 8%; Iron 0% **Exchanges:** ½ Medium-Fat Meat **Carbohydrate Choices:** 0

You can also use regular cream cheese spread instead of the garden vegetable flavor. Just make sure it is the reduced-fat variety, which is softer and spreads more easily than regular cream cheese.

Sausage Cheese Balls

Prep Time: 10 Minutes • Start to Finish: 35 Minutes • About 4 dozen appetizers

¾ cup Bisquick® Gluten Free mix

4 oz bulk gluten-free pork sausage

1½ cups gluten-free shredded Cheddar cheese (6 oz)

¼ cup gluten-free grated Parmesan cheese

¼ teaspoon garlic powder

¼ teaspoon dried rosemary leaves, crushed

⅛ teaspoon ground red pepper (cayenne)

½ cup milk

2 tablespoons chopped fresh parsley

Gluten-free barbecue sauce or chili sauce, if desired

1 Heat oven to 350°F. Spray 15x10x1-inch pan with cooking spray (without flour).

2 In large bowl, mix all ingredients except barbecue sauce. Shape mixture into 1-inch balls. Place in pan.

3 Bake uncovered 22 to 26 minutes or until light golden brown. Immediately remove from pan. Serve warm with sauce for dipping.

1 Appetizer: Calories 30 (Calories from Fat 15); Total Fat 1.5g (Saturated Fat 1g; Trans Fat 0g); Cholesterol 5mg; Sodium 60mg; Total Carbohydrate 2g (Dietary Fiber 0g); Protein 1g **% Daily Value:** Vitamin A 0%; Vitamin C 0%; Calcium 4%; Iron 0% **Exchanges:** ½ Fat **Carbohydrate Choices:** 0

You can use gluten-free turkey sausage as a substitute for the pork sausage.

Sesame Crackers

Prep Time: 45 Minutes • Start to Finish: 1 Hour • 24 crackers

½ cup raw sesame seed

¼ cup white rice flour

¼ cup sweet white sorghum flour

¼ cup brown rice flour

2 tablespoons potato starch flour

¼ teaspoon xanthan gum

½ teaspoon salt

⅛ teaspoon gluten-free baking powder

½ cup roasted sesame tahini

2 tablespoons sunflower or canola oil

6 tablespoons hot water

2 teaspoons gluten-free tamari sauce

1 egg white, beaten

1 Heat oven to 350°F. Spread sesame seed in ungreased shallow pan. Bake uncovered 8 to 10 minutes, stirring occasionally, until golden brown. Set aside to cool.

2 Increase oven temperature to 400°F. Line cookie sheet with cooking parchment paper; spray paper with cooking spray (without flour).

3 In small bowl, mix flours, xanthan gum, salt and baking powder with whisk; set aside. In medium microwavable bowl, microwave tahini, oil and hot water on High 5 seconds; stir with whisk until blended. Add tamari and flour mixture; stir until blended. Reserve 2 tablespoons toasted sesame seed for topping. Stir remaining sesame seed into dough.

4 Spray hands and rolling pin with cooking spray (without flour). Roll dough to ¼-inch thickness. Using small (about 2-inch) cookie cutters, cut dough into shapes, rerolling dough as necessary. Place crackers on cookie sheet; prick with fork. Brush egg white over tops of crackers; sprinkle with reserved sesame seed.

5 Bake 12 to 14 minutes or until golden brown. Immediately remove from cookie sheet to cooling rack.

1 Serving: Calories 80 (Calories from Fat 50); Total Fat 6g (Saturated Fat 1g; Trans Fat 0g); Cholesterol 0mg; Sodium 90mg; Total Carbohydrate 6g (Dietary Fiber 1g); Protein 2g **% Daily Value:** Vitamin A 0%; Vitamin C 0%; Calcium 2%; Iron 4% **Exchanges:** ½ Starch, 1 Fat **Carbohydrate Choices:** ½

Contributed by Jean Duane Alternative Cook http://www.alternativecook.com

Poking holes through the crackers, called "docking," is an important step—it makes the crackers crisp. Cooking supply stores sell a tool called a "docker" (also called "dough prickler"), which is a roller made especially to poke holes in crackers and other doughs.

Poppy Seed Crackers

Prep Time: 30 Minutes • Start to Finish: 45 Minutes • 28 crackers

¾ cup almond flour

¼ cup white rice flour

¼ cup sweet white sorghum flour

¼ cup brown rice flour

2 tablespoons potato starch flour

¼ teaspoon xanthan gum

¼ cup cornstarch

½ teaspoon salt

⅛ teaspoon gluten-free baking powder

⅓ cup sunflower or olive oil

⅓ cup water

½ teaspoon garlic powder

½ teaspoon onion powder

2 tablespoons poppy seed

1 Heat oven to 400°F. Line cookie sheet with cooking parchment paper; spray paper with cooking spray (without flour).

2 In medium bowl, mix flours, xanthan gum, cornstarch, salt and baking powder with whisk. Add remaining ingredients; mix until dough forms a ball.

3 On large non-wooden cutting board sprayed with cooking spray (without flour), roll dough into 14x8-inch rectangle. Cut into 28 (2-inch) squares. With pancake turner, carefully lift squares onto cookie sheet.

4 Bake 12 to 14 minutes or until set. Immediately remove from cookie sheet to cooling rack.

1 Serving: Calories 70 (Calories from Fat 40); Total Fat 4.5g (Saturated Fat 0g; Trans Fat 0g); Cholesterol 0mg; Sodium 25mg; Total Carbohydrate 6g (Dietary Fiber 0g); Protein 1g **% Daily Value:** Vitamin A 0%; Vitamin C 0%; Calcium 0%; Iron 0% **Exchanges:** ½ Starch, 1 Fat **Carbohydrate Choices:** ½

Contributed by Jean Duane Alternative Cook http://www.alternativecook.com

With gluten-free dough, flouring the work surface just doesn't work as well as using cooking spray.

Almond flour (also called "almond meal") is simply raw blanched whole almonds that have been ground into a fine powder.

Bacon-Wrapped Figs

easy quick lowfat

Prep Time: 15 Minutes • Start to Finish: 25 Minutes • 30 appetizers

1 package (12 oz) fully cooked gluten-free cottage or Canadian-style bacon

2 packages (8 oz each) dried whole Calimyrna figs, stems removed

30 pistachio nuts

30 small fresh basil leaves

1 Heat oven to 425°F. Spray 15x10x1-inch pan with cooking spray (without flour). Cut each bacon slice in half.

2 Cut slit in each fig; stuff with nut. Place basil leaf on bacon strip; wrap around fig. Place seam side down in pan.

3 Bake 8 to 10 minutes or until bacon is brown. Serve warm with toothpicks.

1 Appetizer: Calories 70 (Calories from Fat 10); Total Fat 1.5g (Saturated Fat 0g; Trans Fat 0g); Cholesterol 5mg; Sodium 180mg; Total Carbohydrate 10g (Dietary Fiber 1g); Protein 3g **% Daily Value:** Vitamin A 0%; Vitamin C 0%; Calcium 2%; Iron 2% **Exchanges:** ½ Starch, ½ Fat **Carbohydrate Choices:** ½

Calimyrna figs are large, squat, green-skinned, white-fleshed figs grown in California. You can use dried apricot or peach halves, folding them in half around the nut, instead of the figs.

Cottage bacon is taken from smoked pork shoulder. Although it is a leaner form of bacon, it does have more fat and more flavor than Canadian-style bacon.

Amaretto Cheese–Filled Apricots

Prep Time: 30 Minutes • Start to Finish: 1 Hour 30 Minutes • 30 apricots

4 oz cream cheese (half of 8-oz package), softened

⅓ cup slivered almonds, toasted, chopped

¼ cup chopped dried cherries or sweetened dried cranberries

2 tablespoons amaretto

30 soft whole dried apricots

1 In small bowl, mix cream cheese, almonds, the cherries and amaretto with spoon. Spoon into small resealable food-storage plastic bag. Cut ½ inch off a corner of bag.

2 With fingers, open apricots along one side so they look like partially open clamshells. Pipe about 1 teaspoon cheese mixture into each apricot.

3 Refrigerate 1 hour before serving to chill.

1 Apricot: Calories 45 (Calories from Fat 20); Total Fat 2g (Saturated Fat 1g; Trans Fat 0g); Cholesterol 0mg; Sodium 10mg; Total Carbohydrate 6g (Dietary Fiber 0g); Protein 0g **% Daily Value:** Vitamin A 6%; Vitamin C 0%; Calcium 0%; Iron 0% **Exchanges:** ½ Fruit, ½ Fat **Carbohydrate Choices:** ½

These filled apricots would be a beautiful addition to a cheese, fruit and nut platter.

Greek Salad Kabobs

Prep Time: 15 Minutes • Start to Finish: 15 Minutes • 24 servings (1 kabob and ½ tablespoon dip)

DIP

- ¾ **cup plain yogurt**
- 2 **teaspoons honey**
- 2 **teaspoons chopped fresh dill weed**
- 2 **teaspoons chopped fresh oregano leaves**
- ¼ **teaspoon salt**
- 1 **small clove garlic, finely chopped**

KABOBS

- 24 **cocktail picks or toothpicks**
- 24 **pitted kalamata olives**
- 24 **small grape tomatoes**
- 12 **slices (½ inch) English (seedless) cucumber, cut in half crosswise**

1 In small bowl, mix dip ingredients; set aside.

2 On each cocktail pick, thread 1 olive, 1 tomato and 1 half-slice cucumber. Serve kabobs with dip.

1 Serving: Calories 15 (Calories from Fat 5); Total Fat 0.5g (Saturated Fat 0g; Trans Fat 0g); Cholesterol 0mg; Sodium 70mg; Total Carbohydrate 2g (Dietary Fiber 0g); Protein 0g **% Daily Value:** Vitamin A 0%; Vitamin C 2%; Calcium 2%; Iron 0% **Exchanges:** Free **Carbohydrate Choices:** 0

You can use regular cucumber—if the skin is thick or has been coated with a vegetable coating, you may want to peel it.

Zesty Deviled Eggs

Prep Time: 10 Minutes • Start to Finish: 10 Minutes • 12 servings

6 hard-cooked eggs

½ cup gluten-free finely shredded Cheddar cheese (2 oz)

2 tablespoons chopped fresh parsley

3 tablespoons gluten-free mayonnaise, salad dressing or half-and-half

1 teaspoon prepared horseradish

½ teaspoon ground mustard

⅛ teaspoon salt

¼ teaspoon pepper

Tiny cooked shrimp, sliced olives or sliced pimiento, if desired

1 Peel eggs; cut lengthwise in half. Slip out yolks into small bowl; mash with fork. Mix yolks and remaining ingredients except shrimp, olives or pimiento.

2 Fill egg whites with egg yolk mixture, heaping lightly. Garnish with shrimp, olives or pimiento.

1 Serving: Calories 80 (Calories from Fat 60); Total Fat 7g (Saturated Fat 2g; Trans Fat 0g); Cholesterol 110mg; Sodium 105mg; Total Carbohydrate 0g (Dietary Fiber 0g); Protein 4g **% Daily Value:** Vitamin A 4%; Vitamin C 0%; Calcium 4%; Iron 2% **Exchanges:** ½ Medium-Fat Meat, 1 Fat **Carbohydrate Choices:** 0

Top each egg with a small sprig of dill weed just before serving; you can cover and refrigerate the eggs up to 2 days.

Italian Chex® Mix

Prep Time: 10 Minutes • Start to Finish: 50 Minutes • 32 servings (½ cup each)

8 cups Rice Chex® cereal

½ cup salted soy nuts (roasted soybeans)

3 tablespoons olive or canola oil

3 tablespoons balsamic vinegar

2 teaspoons garlic powder

2 teaspoons gluten-free Italian seasoning

1 bag (3 oz) gluten-free fat-free butter-flavor microwave popcorn, popped

⅓ cup gluten-free shredded or grated Parmesan cheese

1 Heat oven to 300°F. In large bowl, mix cereal and soy nuts.

2 In small bowl, mix oil, vinegar, garlic powder and Italian seasoning. Pour over cereal mixture, stirring to coat. Stir in popcorn until well mixed. Spread in ungreased large roasting pan.

3 Bake uncovered 15 minutes. Stir in cheese until well mixed. Bake 10 to 15 minutes longer or until mixture is toasted. Spread on waxed paper; cool about 10 minutes. (Cereal will crisp as it cools.) Store in airtight container.

1 Serving: Calories 60 (Calories from Fat 20); Total Fat 2g (Saturated Fat 0g; Trans Fat 0g); Cholesterol 0mg; Sodium 105mg; Total Carbohydrate 8g (Dietary Fiber 0g); Protein 1g **% Daily Value:** Vitamin A 2%; Vitamin C 0%; Calcium 4%; Iron 15% **Exchanges:** ½ Starch, ½ Fat **Carbohydrate Choices:** ½

Popcorn and Rice Chex® cereal make a savory gluten-free snack that's loaded with whole grain goodness.

Chili and Garlic Snack Mix

Prep Time: 10 Minutes • Start to Finish: 35 Minutes • 32 servings (½ cup each)

8 cups Rice Chex® cereal

1 bag (3 oz) gluten-free fat-free butter-flavor microwave popcorn, popped

¼ cup dry-roasted peanuts

3 tablespoons canola or vegetable oil

⅓ cup gluten-free grated Parmesan cheese

2 teaspoons chili powder

2 teaspoons garlic powder

1 Heat oven to 300°F. In very large bowl, mix cereal, popcorn and peanuts. Drizzle with oil; toss until evenly coated.

2 In small bowl, mix remaining ingredients; sprinkle over cereal mixture. Toss until evenly coated. Spread cereal mixture in ungreased large roasting pan.

3 Bake uncovered 15 minutes, stirring once. Spread on waxed paper; cool about 10 minutes. Store in airtight container.

1 Serving: Calories 60 (Calories from Fat 20); Total Fat 2.5g (Saturated Fat 0g; Trans Fat 0g); Cholesterol 0mg; Sodium 110mg; Total Carbohydrate 8g (Dietary Fiber 0g); Protein 1g **% Daily Value:** Vitamin A 4%; Vitamin C 0%; Calcium 4%; Iron 15% **Exchanges:** ½ Starch, ½ Fat **Carbohydrate Choices:** ½

For an anytime snack, prepare this tasty mix up to 1 week before serving, and store in an airtight container.

Berry Smoothies

Prep Time: 5 Minutes • Start to Finish: 5 Minutes • 2 servings

1 cup frozen unsweetened blueberries or raspberries

1¼ cups vanilla soymilk

1 container (6 oz) Yoplait® Original 99% Fat Free French vanilla yogurt

Honey, if desired

1 In blender or food processor, place blueberries, soymilk and yogurt.

2 Cover; blend on high speed about 1 minute or until smooth. Sweeten to taste with honey. Pour into 2 glasses. Serve immediately.

1 Serving: Calories 210 (Calories from Fat 30); Total Fat 3.5g (Saturated Fat 1g; Trans Fat 0g); Cholesterol 5mg; Sodium 150mg; Total Carbohydrate 37g (Dietary Fiber 3g); Protein 6g **% Daily Value:** Vitamin A 15%; Vitamin C 4%; Calcium 30%; Iron 4% **Exchanges:** ½ Fruit, 1 Other Carbohydrate, 1 Skim Milk, ½ Fat **Carbohydrate Choices:** 2½

Yogurt and soymilk combine to make a calcium-rich gluten-free sipper that will please everyone on a warm day.

Raspberry Lemonade Smoothies

Prep Time: 10 Minutes • Start to Finish: 10 Minutes • 4 servings (1 cup each)

1 cup refrigerated raspberry lemonade (from 64-oz container)

2 ripe bananas, thickly sliced

1½ cups fresh raspberries

2 containers (6 oz each) Yoplait® Original 99% Fat Free red raspberry yogurt

1 In blender or food processor, place all ingredients.

2 Cover; blend on high speed about 1 minute or until smooth and creamy. Pour into glasses. Serve immediately.

1 Serving: Calories 180 (Calories from Fat 15); Total Fat 1.5g (Saturated Fat 0.5g; Trans Fat 0g); Cholesterol 0mg; Sodium 50mg; Total Carbohydrate 42g (Dietary Fiber 5g); Protein 5g **% Daily Value:** Vitamin A 2%; Vitamin C 35%; Calcium 15%; Iron 4% **Exchanges:** 1 Fruit, 1½ Other Carbohydrate, ½ Skim Milk **Carbohydrate Choices:** 2½

Don't have the fresh raspberries? Use frozen raspberries that are slightly thawed instead. Float a few fresh raspberries on top of each smoothie.

Ginger-Rice Crunch

Prep Time: 10 Minutes • Start to Finish: 1 Hour 15 Minutes • 24 servings (½ cup each)

¼ cup packed brown sugar

¼ cup butter or margarine

¼ cup honey

1½ teaspoons ground ginger
or cardamom

6 cups Rice Chex® cereal

1 cup dried banana chips

1 cup unblanched whole almonds

1 cup flaked coconut

½ cup sweetened dried cranberries
or dried pineapple

1 Heat oven to 250°F. Spray large roasting pan with cooking spray (without flour). In 1-quart saucepan, heat brown sugar, butter, honey and ginger to boiling. Remove from heat; cool slightly.

2 Into roasting pan, measure cereal, banana chips, almonds and coconut. Stir in brown sugar mixture until evenly coated.

3 Bake 50 minutes, stirring every 15 minutes. Spread on waxed paper or foil; cool about 15 minutes. Place in serving bowl; stir in cranberries. Store in airtight container.

1 Serving: Calories 140 (Calories from Fat 70); Total Fat 7g (Saturated Fat 3.5g; Trans Fat 0g); Cholesterol 5mg; Sodium 85mg; Total Carbohydrate 18g (Dietary Fiber 1g); Protein 2g **% Daily Value:** Vitamin A 4%; Vitamin C 0%; Calcium 4%; Iron 15% **Exchanges:** ½ Starch, ½ Other Carbohydrate, 1½ Fat **Carbohydrate Choices:** 1

Rice Chex® is a gluten-free breakfast cereal that makes a nutritious snack mix combined with dried fruits and nuts.

For easy cleanup, line the pan with nonstick foil instead of using cooking spray.

Fruiti Sushi

Prep Time: 20 Minutes • Start to Finish: 30 Minutes • 16 candies

1¼ cups Rice Chex® cereal

1 cup white vanilla baking chips

4 rolls Betty Crocker® Fruit Roll-Ups® chewy fruit snack (any favorite flavor; from 5-oz box), unwrapped

12 candy worms

1 Place cereal in resealable food-storage plastic bag; seal bag and crush with fingers to make ¾ cup.

2 In medium microwavable bowl, microwave baking chips as directed on package until melted and stirred smooth. Add crushed cereal; stir until well coated.

3 Unroll fruit snack rolls. For each sushi roll, spread ¼ of cereal mixture on snack roll to within ½ inch of one short side. Arrange 3 candy worms, side by side, on cereal-covered short side.

4 Starting with short side topped with candy worms, roll up each snack roll tightly, pressing unfilled short side of roll to seal. Let sushi rolls stand 5 to 10 minutes or until firm. Cut each roll into 4 slices. Store loosely covered.

1 Candy: Calories 110 (Calories from Fat 35); Total Fat 4g (Saturated Fat 3g; Trans Fat 0g); Cholesterol 0mg; Sodium 65mg; Total Carbohydrate 19g (Dietary Fiber 0g); Protein 1g **% Daily Value:** Vitamin A 0%; Vitamin C 8%; Calcium 2%; Iron 4% **Exchanges:** ½ Starch, ½ Other Carbohydrate, 1 Fat **Carbohydrate Choices:** 1

Arrange sushi pieces on a disposable plate and overwrap with plastic wrap, stretching tightly across the top to look like sushi from the grocery store.

breakfast

Blueberry Pancakes

Prep Time: 20 Minutes • Start to Finish: 20 Minutes • 4 servings (3 pancakes and ¼ cup syrup each)

1 **cup Bisquick® Gluten Free mix**

⅓ **cup Yoplait® Greek Fat Free plain yogurt**

¾ **cup milk**

2 **tablespoons packed brown sugar**

1 **egg, beaten**

1 **teaspoon grated orange peel**

1 **cup fresh blueberries**

1 **cup gluten-free blueberry or maple syrup**

1 Spray griddle with cooking spray (without flour); heat to 375°F. In medium bowl, stir Bisquick mix, yogurt, milk, brown sugar, egg and orange peel until blended. Stir in blueberries.

2 Pour batter by ¼ cupfuls onto hot griddle. Cook until pancakes are bubbly on top, puffed and dry around edges. Turn and cook other sides until golden brown. Serve pancakes with syrup.

1 Serving: Calories 430 (Calories from Fat 20); Total Fat 2.5g (Saturated Fat 0.5g; Trans Fat 0g); Cholesterol 55mg; Sodium 400mg; Total Carbohydrate 96g (Dietary Fiber 1g); Protein 6g **% Daily Value:** Vitamin A 6%; Vitamin C 4%; Calcium 20%; Iron 8% **Exchanges:** 2 Starch, 4½ Other Carbohydrate **Carbohydrate Choices:** 6½

Blueberries owe their blue color to antioxidants called anthocyanins that may help protect cells from oxidation.

Frozen blueberries can be used instead of fresh, or try frozen raspberries. Thaw completely and pat dry with a paper towel; carefully stir into batter.

Applesauce Pancakes with Warm Apple-Cinnamon Topping

Prep Time: 30 Minutes • Start to Finish: 30 Minutes • 3 servings (3 pancakes and ⅔ cup topping each)

TOPPING

2 tablespoons butter

1 large apple, peeled, coarsely chopped (about 1½ cups)

½ teaspoon ground cinnamon

1 cup water

¼ cup packed brown sugar

1 tablespoon cornstarch

1 tablespoon water

PANCAKES

1 cup Bisquick® Gluten Free mix

⅔ cup milk

1 egg

½ cup applesauce

2 tablespoons packed brown sugar

½ teaspoon ground cinnamon

1 In 10-inch skillet, melt butter over medium heat. Stir in apple and ½ teaspoon cinnamon; cook 5 minutes. Add 1 cup water and ¼ cup brown sugar. Heat to boiling; reduce heat. Cover; simmer 10 to 15 minutes, stirring occasionally, until apples are tender. In small bowl, mix cornstarch and 1 tablespoon water; stir into apple mixture. Heat to boiling; boil 1 minute. Remove from heat; keep warm.

2 Spray griddle with cooking spray (without flour); heat to 375°F. In medium bowl, stir pancake ingredients until blended.

3 Pour batter by slightly less than ¼ cupfuls onto hot griddle. Cook until pancakes are bubbly on top, puffed and dry around edges. Turn and cook other sides until golden brown. Serve pancakes with warm topping.

1 Serving: Calories 440 (Calories from Fat 100); Total Fat 11g (Saturated Fat 6g; Trans Fat 0g); Cholesterol 95mg; Sodium 560mg; Total Carbohydrate 81g (Dietary Fiber 3g); Protein 6g **% Daily Value:** Vitamin A 10%; Vitamin C 4%; Calcium 15%; Iron 4% **Exchanges:** 2 Starch, ½ Fruit, 3 Other Carbohydrate, 2 Fat **Carbohydrate Choices:** 5½

The topping can be made a day ahead and warmed just before serving. If you don't want to open a large jar of applesauce, it is available in snack-size containers.

Orange-Cranberry Cinnamon Chex® Breakfast Bars

Prep Time: 20 Minutes • Start to Finish: 1 Hour 20 Minutes • 8 bars

3 cups Cinnamon Chex® cereal

¼ cup tapioca flour

3 tablespoons sweet white sorghum flour

½ teaspoon xanthan gum

⅛ teaspoon salt

⅓ cup sunflower oil

3 eggs

⅓ cup packed brown sugar

1 teaspoon pure vanilla

1 tablespoon grated orange peel

¾ cup sweetened dried cranberries

½ cup slivered almonds, if desired

1 Heat oven to 350°F. Spray 8-inch square pan with cooking spray (without flour).

2 In medium bowl, measure 2½ cups of the cereal. Crush with bottom of measuring cup until finely crushed and measures about 1½ cups; set aside. In small bowl, mix flours, xanthan gum and salt with whisk; set aside.

3 In another medium bowl, beat oil, eggs, brown sugar and vanilla with electric mixer on medium speed until well blended. Gradually add flour mixture, beating until blended. Stir in crushed cereal, orange peel, cranberries and almonds. Press mixture in pan. Coarsely crush remaining ½ cup cereal; sprinkle over top.

4 Bake 25 to 30 minutes or until light golden brown. Cool in pan on cooling rack 30 minutes. Cut into 4 rows by 2 rows.

1 Bar: Calories 270 (Calories from Fat 110); Total Fat 12g (Saturated Fat 1.5g; Trans Fat 0g); Cholesterol 80mg; Sodium 160mg; Total Carbohydrate 37g (Dietary Fiber 1g); Protein 3g **% Daily Value:** Vitamin A 10%; Vitamin C 4%; Calcium 6%; Iron 25% **Exchanges:** 1 Starch, 1½ Other Carbohydrate, 2½ Fat **Carbohydrate Choices:** 2½

Contributed by Jean Duane Alternative Cook http://www.alternativecook.com

Try substituting Honey Nut Chex® for the Cinnamon Chex® and raisins for the dried cranberries.

Sunflower oil is produced from oil-type sunflower seeds. It is lighter in taste and appearance, with lower saturated fat levels than other vegetable oils.

Waffles

Prep Time: 5 Minutes • Start to Finish: 25 Minutes • 4 (6½-inch) waffles

2 eggs

½ cup gluten-free almond, rice, soy or regular milk

3 tablespoons sunflower oil or melted ghee

¼ cup sugar

2 teaspoons pure vanilla

½ cup tapioca flour

½ cup white rice flour

½ cup sorghum flour

2 tablespoons garbanzo and fava flour

2 tablespoons potato starch flour

½ teaspoon gluten-free baking powder

½ teaspoon salt

¼ teaspoon baking soda

1 cup gluten-free maple-flavored syrup

1 Heat waffle maker as directed by manufacturer. In blender, place eggs, milk, oil, sugar and vanilla. Cover; blend until mixed. Add all flours, baking powder, salt and baking soda; blend until well mixed.

2 Pour batter by slightly less than 1 cupful onto center of hot waffle maker. Bake about 5 minutes or until browned on both sides. Remove from waffle maker. Serve immediately with syrup.

1 Waffle and ¼ cup syrup: Calories 640 (Calories from Fat 130); Total Fat 15g (Saturated Fat 2.5g; Trans Fat 0g); Cholesterol 110mg; Sodium 490mg; Total Carbohydrate 117g (Dietary Fiber 2g); Protein 8g **% Daily Value:** Vitamin A 4%; Vitamin C 0%; Calcium 15%; Iron 15% **Exchanges:** 3 Starch, 5 Other Carbohydrate, 2½ Fat **Carbohydrate Choices:** 8

Contributed by Jean Duane Alternative Cook http://www.alternativecook.com

To make pancakes, heat oiled griddle or skillet over high heat. Pour enough batter onto griddle to make 5-inch pancakes. Reduce heat to medium-high; cook until bubbles appear around outer edges of pancakes. Turn pancakes; cook until golden brown on both sides.

Garbanzo bean and fava flour is also called "garbanzo fava bean flour" or "garfava flour."

Apple Cake

Prep Time: 20 Minutes · Start to Finish: 1 Hour 40 Minutes · 12 servings

1 box Betty Crocker® Gluten Free
  yellow cake mix

6 tablespoons cold butter

¼ cup sugar

¼ teaspoon ground cinnamon

2 large tart apples, peeled, sliced

1 container (8 oz) gluten-free
  sour cream

1 teaspoon pure vanilla

2 eggs, lightly beaten

¼ cup sliced almonds

  Sweetened whipped cream,
  if desired

1 Heat oven to 350°F (325°F for dark or nonstick pan). Spray 9-inch square pan with cooking spray (without flour).

2 In medium bowl, place cake mix. Cut in butter, using pastry blender (or pulling 2 table knives through mix in opposite directions), until crumbly. Reserve ½ cup crumb mixture. Press remaining mixture onto bottom and ¾ inch up sides of pan. Bake 10 minutes.

3 Meanwhile, in another medium bowl, mix sugar and cinnamon. Add apples; stir until coated. Spoon apple mixture over hot crust. In small bowl, mix sour cream, vanilla and eggs; drizzle over apples. Bake 40 minutes.

4 In another small bowl, mix almonds and reserved crumb mixture; sprinkle over cake. Bake 15 minutes longer or until apples are tender and topping is light golden brown. Cool on cooling rack at least 15 minutes. Cut into 4 rows by 3 rows. Serve warm with sweetened whipped cream.

1 Serving: Calories 280 (Calories from Fat 100); Total Fat 11g (Saturated Fat 6g; Trans Fat 0g); Cholesterol 60mg; Sodium 260mg; Total Carbohydrate 41g (Dietary Fiber 0g); Protein 3g **% Daily Value:** Vitamin A 8%; Vitamin C 0%; Calcium 4%; Iron 0% **Exchanges:** 1 Starch, 1½ Other Carbohydrate, 2 Fat **Carbohydrate Choices:** 3

Substitute sliced fresh peaches for the apples or stir in ¼ cup dried currants or cranberries with the apples.

Hazelnut Streusel Coffee Cake

Prep Time: 20 Minutes • Start to Finish: 50 Minutes • 9 servings

½ cup packed brown sugar

⅓ cup hazelnut spread with cocoa

½ cup chopped hazelnuts (filberts)

¼ cup miniature semisweet chocolate chips

1¼ cups Gluten-Free All-Purpose Flour Blend (page 15)

1½ teaspoons gluten-free baking powder

¼ teaspoon salt

3 eggs

½ cup granulated sugar

½ cup butter, melted

2 teaspoons pure vanilla

1 Heat oven to 350°F. Spray 8-inch square pan with cooking spray (without flour).

2 In small bowl, mix brown sugar and hazelnut spread. Stir in hazelnuts and chocolate chips; set aside for topping.

3 In large bowl, stir flour blend, baking powder and salt; set aside. In medium bowl, beat eggs and granulated sugar with whisk until smooth. Stir in butter and vanilla. Stir into flour mixture just until combined. Pour batter into pan. Sprinkle with reserved topping mixture.

4 Bake 25 to 27 minutes or until toothpick inserted in center comes out clean. Serve warm.

1 Serving: Calories 410 (Calories from Fat 190); Total Fat 21g (Saturated Fat 9g; Trans Fat 0g); Cholesterol 100mg; Sodium 350mg; Total Carbohydrate 49g (Dietary Fiber 2g); Protein 5g **% Daily Value:** Vitamin A 8%; Vitamin C 0%; Calcium 10%; Iron 8% **Exchanges:** 1½ Starch, 2 Other Carbohydrate, 4 Fat **Carbohydrate Choices:** 3

Contributed by Silvana Nardone Silvana's Kitchen http://silvanaskitchen.com

Hazelnuts, from the hazel tree, are a good source of vitamin E and trace minerals such as selenium, manganese and copper, which are essential for cell function.

Fruit Swirl Coffee Cake

Prep Time: 20 Minutes • Start to Finish: 45 Minutes • 18 servings

COFFEE CAKE

4 **eggs**

¾ **cup milk**

½ **cup butter, melted**

2 **teaspoons pure vanilla**

1 **box Bisquick® Gluten Free mix (3 cups)**

⅔ **cup granulated sugar**

1 **can (21 oz) gluten-free fruit pie filling (any flavor)**

GLAZE

1 **cup gluten-free powdered sugar**

2 **tablespoons milk**

1 Heat oven to 375°F. Grease 1 (15x10x1-inch) pan or 2 (9-inch) square pans with shortening or cooking spray (without flour).

2 In large bowl, stir all coffee cake ingredients except pie filling until blended; beat vigorously 30 seconds. Spread ⅔ of the batter (about 2½ cups) in 15x10-inch pan or ⅓ of the batter (about 1¼ cups) in each square pan.

3 Spread pie filling over batter (filling may not cover batter completely). Drop remaining batter by tablespoonfuls onto pie filling.

4 Bake 20 to 25 minutes or until golden brown. Meanwhile, in small bowl, mix glaze ingredients until smooth. Drizzle glaze over warm coffee cake. Serve warm or cool.

1 Serving: Calories 240 (Calories from Fat 60); Total Fat 7g (Saturated Fat 4g; Trans Fat 0g); Cholesterol 60mg; Sodium 280mg; Total Carbohydrate 41g (Dietary Fiber 0g); Protein 3g **% Daily Value:** Vitamin A 6%; Vitamin C 0%; Calcium 4%; Iron 0% **Exchanges:** 1 Starch, 1½ Other Carbohydrate, 1½ Fat **Carbohydrate Choices:** 3

This easy fruit-filled coffee cake is ripe for any flavor of filling—take your pick! Try apple, cherry, blueberry, peach or apricot pie filling. Or try gluten-free lemon curd for a luscious citrus twist.

Cinnamon Streusel Coffee Cake

Prep Time: 10 Minutes • Start to Finish: 40 Minutes • 6 servings

STREUSEL TOPPING

⅓ **cup Bisquick® Gluten Free mix**

½ **cup packed brown sugar**

¾ **teaspoon ground cinnamon**

¼ **cup cold butter or margarine**

COFFEE CAKE

1¾ **cup Bisquick® Gluten Free mix**

3 **tablespoons granulated sugar**

⅔ **cup milk or water**

1½ **teaspoons pure vanilla**

3 **eggs**

1 Heat oven to 350°F. Spray 9-inch round or square pan with cooking spray (without flour). In small bowl, mix ⅓ cup Bisquick mix, the brown sugar and cinnamon. Using pastry blender or fork, cut in butter until mixture is crumbly; set aside.

2 In medium bowl, stir all coffee cake ingredients until blended. Spread in pan; sprinkle with topping.

3 Bake 25 to 30 minutes or until golden brown. Store tightly covered.

1 Serving: Calories 380 (Calories from Fat 100); Total Fat 11g (Saturated Fat 6g; Trans Fat 0g); Cholesterol 130mg; Sodium 570mg; Total Carbohydrate 62g (Dietary Fiber 1g); Protein 6g **% Daily Value:** Vitamin A 8%; Vitamin C 0%; Calcium 10%; Iron 2% **Exchanges:** 2 Starch, 2 Other Carbohydrate, 2 Fat **Carbohydrate Choices:** 4

This coffee cake is perfect for brunch. Add a bowl of cut-up fresh fruit drizzled with poppy seed dressing and a plate of sliced cheeses to complete the menu.

Eggnog Breakfast Cake

Prep Time: 30 Minutes • Start to Finish: 2 Hours 10 Minutes • 10 servings

1 box Betty Crocker® Gluten Free yellow cake mix

⅔ cup milk

½ cup butter, softened

1½ teaspoons rum extract

1 teaspoon pure vanilla

¼ teaspoon ground nutmeg

3 eggs

¼ cup Betty Crocker® Rich & Creamy vanilla frosting

⅓ cup chopped pecans

1 Heat oven to 350°F (or 325°F for dark or nonstick pan). Grease bottom only of 8- or 9-inch round or square pan. In large bowl, beat cake mix, milk, butter, rum extract, vanilla, nutmeg and eggs with electric mixer on low speed 30 seconds, then on medium speed 2 minutes, scraping bowl occasionally. Pour into pan.

2 Bake 33 to 41 minutes or until toothpick inserted in center comes out clean. Cool 10 minutes. Run knife around inside edge of pan. Cool on cooling rack 30 minutes longer.

3 Heat frosting in microwavable bowl on High 10 to 15 seconds or until easy to drizzle. Drizzle frosting over cake; sprinkle with pecans.

1 Serving: Calories 320 (Calories from Fat 130); Total Fat 15g (Saturated Fat 7g; Trans Fat 1g); Cholesterol 90mg; Sodium 340mg; Total Carbohydrate 43g (Dietary Fiber 0g); Protein 4g **% Daily Value:** Vitamin A 8%; Vitamin C 0%; Calcium 4%; Iron 0% **Exchanges:** 1 Starch, 2 Other Carbohydrate, 3 Fat **Carbohydrate Choices:** 3

For an indulgent treat, use candied pecans— just make sure they're gluten-free.

Huevos Rancheros Breakfast Pizza

Prep Time: 25 Minutes • Start to Finish: 45 Minutes • 6 servings

CRUST

- 1 cup Bisquick® Gluten Free mix
- ½ cup cornmeal
- ½ cup water
- 2 eggs, beaten
- 1 cup gluten-free shredded Monterey Jack cheese (4 oz)

TOPPING

- 1 cup Old El Paso® Thick 'n Chunky salsa
- ½ lb gluten-free chorizo or bulk spicy Italian pork sausage
- 6 eggs, beaten
- ½ cup gluten-free shredded Monterey Jack cheese (2 oz)
- 2 tablespoons chopped fresh cilantro

1 Heat oven to 350°F. Spray 12-inch pizza pan with cooking spray (without flour).

2 In medium bowl, stir Bisquick mix, cornmeal, water and 2 eggs. Add 1 cup cheese; stir until blended. Spread in pan. Bake 15 minutes or until set. Spread ½ cup of the salsa over warm crust.

3 Meanwhile, in 10-inch nonstick skillet, cook chorizo over medium-high heat, stirring frequently, until fully cooked. Remove to small bowl; set aside. Wipe out skillet. Add 6 eggs to skillet; cook over medium-low heat until almost set (eggs will still be moist). Gently stir chorizo into eggs. Spoon mixture over baked crust, covering completely. Sprinkle with ½ cup cheese.

4 Bake 5 minutes or until cheese is melted. Sprinkle with cilantro. Serve with remaining ½ cup salsa.

1 Serving: Calories 430 (Calories from Fat 210); Total Fat 24g (Saturated Fat 10g; Trans Fat 0g); Cholesterol 325mg; Sodium 950mg; Total Carbohydrate 31g (Dietary Fiber 1g); Protein 22g **% Daily Value:** Vitamin A 15%; Vitamin C 0%; Calcium 30%; Iron 10% **Exchanges:** 2 Starch, 2½ Medium-Fat Meat, 2 Fat **Carbohydrate Choices:** 2

Chorizo is a spicy pork sausage containing Mexican seasonings such as chili powder and cumin. If you are unable to find it, any other gluten-free spicy pork sausage would make a good substitution.

Breakfast Skillet

Prep Time: 30 Minutes • Start to Finish: 30 Minutes • 4 servings

¾ lb gluten-free bacon, cut into
1-inch pieces

3 cups refrigerated cooked
shredded hash brown potatoes
(from 20-oz bag)

3 eggs

1 can (4.5 oz) green chiles, drained

¾ cup gluten-free shredded
Cheddar cheese (3 oz)

1 medium tomato, seeded, chopped
(¾ cup)

1 In 10-inch nonstick skillet, cook bacon over medium heat
5 to 7 minutes, stirring occasionally, until crisp. Drain, reserving
2 tablespoons drippings and bacon in skillet.

2 Add potatoes; spread evenly in skillet. Cook 8 to 10 minutes,
stirring occasionally, until brown.

3 In small bowl, beat eggs and chiles with fork or whisk. Pour egg
mixture evenly over potatoes. Reduce heat to low; cover and cook
8 to 10 minutes or until eggs are firm. Sprinkle with cheese and tomato;
cover and cook 2 to 4 minutes longer or until cheese is melted.

1 Serving: Calories 380 (Calories from Fat 190); Total Fat 21g (Saturated Fat 9g; Trans Fat 0g); Cholesterol
205mg; Sodium 940mg; Total Carbohydrate 28g (Dietary Fiber 2g); Protein 20g **% Daily Value:** Vitamin A 15%;
Vitamin C 15%; Calcium 15%; Iron 10% **Exchanges:** 2 Starch, ½ Medium-Fat Meat, 1½ High-Fat Meat,
1 Fat **Carbohydrate Choices:** 2

Start the weekend off with a protein-packed
gluten-free breakfast.

For a little more spice, try using pepper Jack
cheese instead of Cheddar.

Home-Style Scrambled Eggs

Prep Time: 10 Minutes • Start to Finish: 20 Minutes • 4 servings

6 **eggs**

¾ **teaspoon salt**

3 **tablespoons water**

¼ **cup butter or margarine**

1 **cup refrigerated diced potatoes with onions or frozen hash brown potatoes**

1 **small zucchini, chopped (1 cup)**

1 **medium tomato, seeded, chopped (¾ cup)**

1 In medium bowl, beat eggs, salt and water. In 10-inch skillet, melt butter over medium heat. Add potatoes, zucchini and tomato; cook, stirring occasionally, until hot.

2 Pour egg mixture over vegetable mixture. As mixture begins to set on bottom and side, gently lift cooked portions with spatula so that thin, uncooked portion can flow to bottom. Do not stir. Cook 3 to 5 minutes or until eggs are thickened throughout but still moist.

1 Serving: Calories 260 (Calories from Fat 180); Total Fat 20g (Saturated Fat 10g; Trans Fat 0g); Cholesterol 350mg; Sodium 690mg; Total Carbohydrate 10g (Dietary Fiber 1g); Protein 11g **% Daily Value:** Vitamin A 20%; Vitamin C 10%; Calcium 4%; Iron 6% **Exchanges:** ½ Starch, ½ Vegetable, 1 Medium-Fat Meat, 3 Fat **Carbohydrate Choices:** ½

Do your scrambled eggs end up looking more like rice or peas than the fluffy, moist, thick eggs from a restaurant? The trick is to stir them as little as possible while they cook.

Artichoke-Basil Frittata

Prep Time: 10 Minutes · Start to Finish: 25 Minutes · 6 servings

1 **can (13 to 14.5 oz) artichoke hearts, drained, or 1 package (12 oz) frozen artichoke hearts, thawed**

1 **tablespoon olive oil**

½ **cup chopped red onion**

2 **cloves garlic, finely chopped**

2 **tablespoons chopped fresh or 2 teaspoons dried basil leaves**

1 **tablespoon chopped fresh parsley**

6 **eggs**

½ **teaspoon salt**

¼ **teaspoon pepper**

2 **tablespoons gluten-free freshly grated Parmesan cheese**

1 Cut artichoke hearts into quarters. In 10-inch ovenproof nonstick skillet, heat oil over medium heat (if not using nonstick skillet, increase oil to 2 tablespoons). Add onion, garlic, basil and parsley; cook 3 minutes, stirring frequently, until onion is tender. Reduce heat to medium-low.

2 In medium bowl, beat eggs, salt and pepper until blended. Pour over onion mixture. Arrange artichokes on top of egg mixture. Cover; cook 7 to 9 minutes or until eggs are set around edge and beginning to brown on bottom (egg mixture will be uncooked on top). Sprinkle with cheese.

3 Set oven control to broil. Broil frittata with top about 5 inches from heat about 3 minutes or until eggs are cooked on top and light golden brown. (Frittata will puff up during broiling but will collapse when removed from broiler.)

1 Serving: Calories 150 (Calories from Fat 80); Total Fat 8g (Saturated Fat 2.5g; Trans Fat 0g); Cholesterol 215mg; Sodium 460mg; Total Carbohydrate 10g (Dietary Fiber 6g); Protein 9g **% Daily Value:** Vitamin A 8%; Vitamin C 6%; Calcium 8%; Iron 6% **Exchanges:** ½ Starch, 1 Medium-Fat Meat, ½ Fat **Carbohydrate Choices:** ½

The cooked egg under the artichoke pieces may turn light green due to the acid in the artichoke hearts—don't worry, this doesn't affect the flavor of the frittata.

Herbed Potato-Egg Scramble

Prep Time: 20 Minutes • Start to Finish: 20 Minutes • 4 servings

- 2 **teaspoons canola oil**
- 1 **medium red potato, unpeeled, cut into ½-inch pieces (¾ to 1 cup)**
- ⅛ **teaspoon salt**
- 3 **tablespoons water**
- 1½ **cups fat-free egg product or 6 eggs**
- ½ **teaspoon dried or 1 teaspoon chopped fresh basil leaves**
- ¼ **cup sliced roasted red bell peppers (from 12-oz jar)**
- 2 **tablespoons gluten-free shredded Parmesan cheese**

1 In 12-inch nonstick skillet, heat oil over medium-high heat. Add potato; sprinkle with salt. Cook 1 to 2 minutes, stirring frequently. Add water; cover and reduce heat to low. Cook 5 to 7 minutes, stirring occasionally, until potato is fork-tender.

2 Meanwhile, in medium bowl, beat egg product and basil with whisk until well blended. Stir in roasted peppers.

3 Pour egg mixture over potato in skillet. Cook over medium-low heat 3 to 5 minutes, stirring frequently, until eggs are set but still moist. Sprinkle with cheese.

1 Serving: Calories 110 (Calories from Fat 30); Total Fat 3.5g (Saturated Fat 1g; Trans Fat 0g); Cholesterol 0mg; Sodium 310mg; Total Carbohydrate 7g (Dietary Fiber 1g); Protein 12g **% Daily Value:** Vitamin A 20%; Vitamin C 15%; Calcium 8%; Iron 10% **Exchanges:** ½ Starch, 1½ Very Lean Meat, ½ Fat **Carbohydrate Choices:** ½

Red potatoes have a slightly waxy texture and retain their shape better when cooked than russet potatoes.

Impossibly Easy Breakfast Bake

Prep Time: 20 Minutes • Start to Finish: 1 Hour 5 Minutes • 12 servings

1 package (16 oz) gluten-free bulk pork sausage

1 medium red bell pepper, chopped (1 cup)

1 medium onion, chopped (½ cup)

3 cups frozen hash brown potatoes

2 cups gluten-free shredded Cheddar cheese (8 oz)

6 eggs

2 cups milk

¾ cup Bisquick® Gluten Free mix

¼ teaspoon pepper

1 Heat oven to 400°F. Spray 13x9-inch (3-quart) glass baking dish with cooking spray (without flour). In 10-inch skillet, cook sausage, bell pepper and onion over medium heat, stirring occasionally, until sausage is no longer pink; drain. In baking dish, mix sausage mixture, potatoes and 1½ cups of the cheese.

2 In medium bowl, stir eggs, milk, Bisquick mix and pepper until blended. Pour over sausage mixture in baking dish.

3 Bake 30 to 35 minutes or until knife inserted in center comes out clean. Sprinkle with remaining ½ cup cheese. Bake about 3 minutes longer or until cheese is melted. Let stand 5 minutes before serving.

1 Serving: Calories 270 (Calories from Fat 130); Total Fat 15g (Saturated Fat 7g; Trans Fat 0g); Cholesterol 145mg; Sodium 520mg; Total Carbohydrate 21g (Dietary Fiber 1g); Protein 14g **% Daily Value:** Vitamin A 15%; Vitamin C 15%; Calcium 20%; Iron 6% **Exchanges:** 1 Starch, 1 Vegetable, 1 High-Fat Meat, 1½ Fat **Carbohydrate Choices:** 1½

Frozen hash browns are available shredded or diced, sometimes called "southern" or "country-style"—either kind will work in this recipe.

Spinach-Mushroom Quiche

Prep Time: 30 Minutes • Start to Finish: 1 Hour 40 Minutes • 8 servings

CRUST

- 1 cup Bisquick® Gluten Free mix
- ⅓ cup plus 1 tablespoon shortening
- 3 to 4 tablespoons cold water

FILLING

- 1 tablespoon butter
- 1 small onion, chopped (⅓ cup)
- 1½ cups sliced fresh mushrooms (about 4 oz)
- 4 eggs
- 1 cup milk
- ⅛ teaspoon ground red pepper (cayenne)
- ¾ cup coarsely chopped fresh spinach
- ¼ cup chopped red bell pepper
- 1 cup gluten-free shredded Italian cheese blend (4 oz)

1 Heat oven to 425°F. In medium bowl, place Bisquick mix. Cut in shortening, using pastry blender (or pulling 2 table knives through ingredients in opposite directions), until particles are size of small peas. Sprinkle with cold water, 1 tablespoon at a time, tossing with fork until all flour is moistened and pastry almost leaves side of bowl (1 to 2 teaspoons more water can be added if necessary).

2 Press pastry in bottom and up side of ungreased 9-inch quiche dish or glass pie plate. Bake 12 to 14 minutes or until crust just begins to brown and is set. Reduce oven temperature to 325°F.

3 Meanwhile, in 10-inch skillet, melt butter over medium heat. Cook onion and mushrooms in butter about 5 minutes, stirring occasionally, until tender. In medium bowl, beat eggs, milk and red pepper until well blended. Stir in spinach, bell pepper, mushroom mixture and cheese. Pour into partially baked crust.

4 Bake 40 to 45 minutes or until knife inserted in center comes out clean. Let stand 10 minutes before cutting.

1 Serving: Calories 260 (Calories from Fat 160); Total Fat 17g (Saturated Fat 6g; Trans Fat 2g); Cholesterol 120mg; Sodium 340mg; Total Carbohydrate 16g (Dietary Fiber 0g); Protein 9g **% Daily Value:** Vitamin A 15%; Vitamin C 6%; Calcium 30%; Iron 2% **Exchanges:** 1 Starch, ½ Vegetable, 1 Medium-Fat Meat, 2 Fat **Carbohydrate Choices:** 1

A 4-oz can of sliced mushrooms (drained) can be substituted for the fresh mushrooms. If you prefer, you can use gluten-free shredded Cheddar or gluten-free shredded Monterey Jack cheese in place of the Italian cheese blend.

Quiche Lorraine

Prep Time: 25 Minutes • Start to Finish: 1 Hour 40 Minutes • 6 servings

PASTRY

⅓ **cup plus 1 tablespoon shortening**

1 **cup Bisquick® Gluten Free mix**

3 **to 4 tablespoons cold water**

FILLING

8 **slices gluten-free bacon, crisply cooked, crumbled (½ cup)**

1 **cup gluten-free shredded Swiss cheese (4 oz)**

⅓ **cup finely chopped onion**

4 **eggs**

2 **cups whipping cream or half-and-half**

¼ **teaspoon salt**

¼ **teaspoon pepper**

⅛ **teaspoon ground red pepper (cayenne)**

1 Heat oven to 425°F. In medium bowl, cut shortening into Bisquick mix, using pastry blender (or pulling 2 table knives through ingredients in opposite directions), until particles are size of small peas. Sprinkle with cold water, 1 tablespoon at a time, tossing with fork until all flour is moistened and pastry almost cleans side of bowl (1 to 2 teaspoons more water can be added if necessary).

2 Gather pastry into a ball. In ungreased 9-inch quiche dish or glass pie plate, press pastry evenly in bottom and up sides. Bake 12 to 14 minutes or until pastry just begins to brown and is set.

3 Reduce oven temperature to 325°F. Sprinkle bacon, cheese and onion into crust. In medium bowl, beat eggs slightly; beat in remaining filling ingredients. Pour into crust.

4 Bake 45 to 50 minutes or until knife inserted in center comes out clean. Cool 10 minutes before serving.

1 Serving: Calories 460 (Calories from Fat 310); Total Fat 34g (Saturated Fat 14g; Trans Fat 3g); Cholesterol 195mg; Sodium 590mg; Total Carbohydrate 23g (Dietary Fiber 0g); Protein 15g **% Daily Value:** Vitamin A 15%; Vitamin C 0%; Calcium 25%; Iron 4% **Exchanges:** 1 Starch, ½ Low-Fat Milk, 1 Medium-Fat Meat, 5 Fat **Carbohydrate Choices:** 1½

For a mushroom quiche, add a 4-ounce can of mushrooms pieces and stems, drained, and a 2-ounce jar of diced pimientos, well drained, with the bacon.

chapter 3

meals

Cheesy Vegetable Pizza with Fresh Basil

Prep Time: 10 Minutes • Start to Finish: 1 Hour 20 Minutes • 2 pizzas (6 servings each)

CRUST

1¾ cups lukewarm water (about 95°F)

2 teaspoons unflavored gelatin

1 tablespoon fast-rising dry yeast

2 tablespoons olive oil

2 tablespoons honey

1 teaspoon apple cider vinegar

1 cup sorghum flour

¾ cup brown rice flour

½ cup garbanzo and fava flour

½ cup white rice flour

½ cup potato starch flour

1 teaspoon salt

1 teaspoon guar gum

1 teaspoon xanthan gum

TOPPINGS

Cooking spray without flour

1 can (15 oz) gluten-free pizza sauce

1 bell pepper, cut into thin slices

1 package (8 oz) sliced mushrooms

¼ cup sliced fresh basil leaves

2 cups gluten-free shredded mozzarella cheese (8 oz)

1 Spray 2 (12-inch) pizza pans with cooking spray (without flour). In small bowl, stir water, gelatin, yeast, oil, honey and vinegar until yeast is dissolved; set aside.

2 In medium bowl, stir together remaining crust ingredients. Add yeast mixture; beat with electric mixer on low speed 1 minute.

3 Divide dough in half. Spread half of dough in each pizza pan. Lightly spray dough with cooking spray; cover with plastic wrap. Let rise in warm place (80°F to 85°F) until doubled in height, about 45 minutes.

4 Heat oven to 425°F. Uncover dough; bake 10 minutes or until surface is dry. Remove from oven. Spread half of pizza sauce over each crust. Top each with half of the remaining toppings, ending with cheese. Bake 15 to 20 minutes longer or until crust is browned and cheese is melted.

1 Serving: Calories 530 (Calories from Fat 140); Total Fat 15g (Saturated Fat 6g; Trans Fat 0g); Cholesterol 20mg; Sodium 740mg; Total Carbohydrate 78g (Dietary Fiber 7g); Protein 21g **% Daily Value:** Vitamin A 15%; Vitamin C 60%; Calcium 35%; Iron 20% **Exchanges:** 3½ Starch, 1 Other Carbohydrate, 2 Vegetable, 1 Very Lean Meat, 2½ Fat **Carbohydrate Choices:** 5

Contributed by Jean Duane Alternative Cook http://www.alternativecook.com

Bell peppers are rich in vitamin C, an essential antioxidant nutrient that helps keep cells healthy by protecting them from oxidation. If you're topping the pizza with bell peppers, or other veggies, chop them and pre-bake them for 20 to 25 minutes before baking them on the pizza.

Quick Pizza

Prep Time: 10 Minutes • Start to Finish: 40 Minutes • 6 servings

PIZZA CRUST

1⅓ cups Bisquick® Gluten Free mix

½ teaspoon gluten-free Italian seasoning or dried basil leaves

½ cup water

⅓ cup vegetable oil

2 eggs, beaten

SUGGESTED TOPPINGS

1 can (8 oz) gluten-free pizza sauce

1 cup bite-size pieces favorite meat or vegetables

1½ cups gluten-free shredded mozzarella cheese (6 oz)

1 Heat oven to 425°F. Grease 12-inch pizza pan with shortening or cooking spray (without flour). In medium bowl, stir Bisquick mix, Italian seasoning, water, oil and eggs until well combined; spread in pan. Bake 15 minutes (crust will appear cracked).

2 Spread pizza sauce over crust; top with meat and cheese. Bake 10 to 15 minutes longer or until cheese is melted.

1 Serving: Calories 230 (Calories from Fat 130); Total Fat 14g (Saturated Fat 2.5g; Trans Fat 0g); Cholesterol 70mg; Sodium 320mg; Total Carbohydrate 23g (Dietary Fiber 0g); Protein 3g **% Daily Value:** Vitamin A 2%; Vitamin C 0%; Calcium 4%; Iron 0% **Exchanges:** 1½ Starch, 2½ Fat **Carbohydrate Choices:** 1½

For a white pizza, brush the crust with olive oil and sprinkle with garlic and herbs. Then, top with chopped cooked chicken and grated Parmesan cheese. Or, spread the crust with gluten-free Alfredo sauce instead of using the oil, garlic and herbs.

Meat Lover's Pizza

Prep Time: 25 Minutes • Start to Finish: 40 Minutes • 6 servings

1⅓ cups Bisquick® Gluten Free mix

1 teaspoon dried basil leaves

½ cup water

⅓ cup vegetable oil

2 eggs, beaten

2 cups gluten-free shredded mozzarella cheese (8 oz)

½ lb gluten-free bulk Italian pork sausage

1 large onion, chopped (1 cup)

1 medium red bell pepper, chopped (1 cup)

1 can (8 oz) gluten-free pizza sauce

2 oz gluten-free sliced pepperoni

1 Heat oven to 425°F. Spray 12-inch pizza pan with cooking spray (without flour).

2 In medium bowl, stir Bisquick mix, basil, water, oil and eggs until well blended. Spread in pan. Sprinkle with ½ cup of the cheese. Bake 15 minutes or until cheese turns golden brown.

3 Meanwhile, in 10-inch skillet, cook sausage, onion and bell pepper over medium heat 8 to 10 minutes, stirring occasionally, until sausage is no longer pink and vegetables are tender. Remove from heat; drain if necessary.

4 Spread pizza sauce over partially baked crust. Top with pepperoni and sausage mixture. Sprinkle with remaining 1½ cups cheese. Bake 10 to 15 minutes or until cheese is melted.

1 Serving: Calories 510 (Calories from Fat 300); Total Fat 34g (Saturated Fat 11g; Trans Fat 0g); Cholesterol 115mg; Sodium 1040mg; Total Carbohydrate 30g (Dietary Fiber 2g); Protein 21g **% Daily Value:** Vitamin A 25%; Vitamin C 30%; Calcium 35%; Iron 6% **Exchanges:** 2 Starch, ½ Vegetable, 2 Medium-Fat Meat, 4½ Fat **Carbohydrate Choices:** 2

For a crisper crust, sprinkle cornmeal on the sprayed pizza pan.

Sprinkle ¼ cup sliced fresh basil leaves over the meat and veggies before topping with cheese.

Creamy Chicken and Broccoli Fettuccine

Prep Time: 30 Minutes • Start to Finish: 30 Minutes • 6 servings (1⅓ cups each)

6 oz uncooked gluten-free fettuccine (from 14-oz package)

1 tablespoon canola oil

1 lb boneless skinless chicken breasts, cut into 1-inch pieces

1 medium onion, chopped (½ cup)

1 teaspoon gluten-free seasoned salt

2 cups fresh broccoli florets

1 package (8 oz) sliced fresh mushrooms (about 3 cups)

1 medium red bell pepper, cut into 2- to 3-inch strips (1 cup)

4 oz (half of 8-oz package) ⅓-less-fat cream cheese (Neufchâtel), cut into cubes

1 teaspoon gluten-free garlic-pepper blend

1 Cook and drain fettuccine as directed on package.

2 Meanwhile, in 12-inch nonstick skillet, heat oil over medium heat. Add chicken and onion; sprinkle with seasoned salt. Cook about 4 minutes, stirring occasionally. Stir in broccoli, mushrooms and bell pepper. Cook 6 to 8 minutes, stirring occasionally, until chicken is no longer pink in center and vegetables are crisp-tender.

3 Add cream cheese and garlic-pepper blend to chicken mixture in skillet; stir to blend. Stir in cooked fettuccine; cook until thoroughly heated.

1 Serving: Calories 300 (Calories from Fat 90); Total Fat 10g (Saturated Fat 3.5g; Trans Fat 0g); Cholesterol 60mg; Sodium 350mg; Total Carbohydrate 29g (Dietary Fiber 1g); Protein 23g **% Daily Value:** Vitamin A 20%; Vitamin C 40%; Calcium 6%; Iron 15% **Exchanges:** 1½ Starch, 1½ Vegetable, 2 Very Lean Meat, 1½ Fat **Carbohydrate Choices:** 2

For a special touch, stir in ¼ cup dry white wine, such as Chardonnay, with the cream cheese.

Ultimate Chicken Fingers

Prep Time: 10 Minutes • Start to Finish: 25 Minutes • 5 servings

¾ cup Bisquick® Gluten Free mix

½ cup gluten-free grated Parmesan cheese (2 oz)

1 teaspoon paprika

½ teaspoon salt or gluten-free garlic salt

3 boneless skinless chicken breasts (1 lb), cut crosswise into ½-inch strips

2 eggs, slightly beaten

3 tablespoons butter or margarine, melted

1 Heat oven to 450°F. Line cookie sheet with foil; spray with cooking spray (without flour).

2 In shallow baking dish, stir together Bisquick mix, cheese, paprika and salt. Dip chicken strips into eggs, then coat with Bisquick mixture; repeat dipping in eggs and Bisquick mixture. Place chicken on cookie sheet. Drizzle butter over chicken.

3 Bake 12 to 14 minutes, turning after 6 minutes, until no longer pink in center.

1 Serving: Calories 310 (Calories from Fat 140); Total Fat 15g (Saturated Fat 8g; Trans Fat 0g); Cholesterol 165mg; Sodium 740mg; Total Carbohydrate 16g (Dietary Fiber 0g); Protein 28g **% Daily Value:** Vitamin A 15%; Vitamin C 0%; Calcium 20%; Iron 6% **Exchanges:** 1 Starch, 3½ Lean Meat, 1 Fat **Carbohydrate Choices:** 1

Try serving these chicken fingers on a bed of salad greens with sliced tomatoes.

Oven-Baked Chicken

1 tablespoon butter or margarine
1 cup Bisquick® Gluten Free mix
1 teaspoon gluten-free seasoned salt
1 teaspoon paprika
½ teaspoon garlic powder
¼ teaspoon pepper
2 eggs, beaten
1 cut-up whole chicken (3 lb)

1 Heat oven to 400°F. In 13x9-inch (3-quart) glass baking dish, melt butter in oven.

2 In medium bowl, stir together Bisquick mix, salt, paprika, garlic powder and pepper. Place eggs in shallow dish. Dip chicken into eggs, then coat with Bisquick mixture; repeat dipping in eggs and Bisquick mixture. Place skin side down in heated dish.

3 Bake 35 minutes. Turn chicken; bake about 15 minutes longer or until juice of chicken is clear when thickest piece is cut to bone (165°F).

1 Serving: Calories 420 (Calories from Fat 190); Total Fat 21g (Saturated Fat 7g; Trans Fat 0.5g); Cholesterol 195mg; Sodium 680mg; Total Carbohydrate 21g (Dietary Fiber 0g); Protein 36g **% Daily Value:** Vitamin A 10%; Vitamin C 0%; Calcium 6%; Iron 10% **Exchanges:** 1½ Starch, 4½ Lean Meat, 1½ Fat **Carbohydrate Choices:** 1½

Serve with sides of steamed veggies—they are great partners for the baked chicken.

Orange-Glazed Roast Turkey with Cranberry-Orange Stuffing

Prep Time: 45 Minutes • Start to Finish: 6 Hours • 12 servings

STUFFING

⅓ **cup butter or margarine**

3 **medium stalks celery, chopped (1½ cups)**

1 **large onion, finely chopped (1 cup)**

8 **cups cornbread cubes**

¾ **cup sweetened dried cranberries**

4½ **teaspoons chopped fresh or 1½ teaspoons dried sage leaves**

2 **teaspoons grated orange peel**

1¼ **cups Progresso® chicken broth (from 32-oz carton)**

½ **cup chopped pecans, toasted**

TURKEY

1 **whole unbasted turkey (12 lb), thawed if frozen**

2 **teaspoons dried sage leaves, crumbled**

1 **teaspoon salt**

¼ **teaspoon pepper**

2 **tablespoons butter, melted**

GLAZE

½ **cup orange marmalade, melted**

1 In 10-inch skillet, melt ⅓ cup butter over medium heat. Cook celery and onion in butter about 3 minutes, stirring occasionally, until crisp-tender. In large bowl, mix cornbread cubes, celery mixture and remaining stuffing ingredients.

2 Heat oven to 325°F. Stuff turkey just before roasting. Fill wishbone area with stuffing. Fasten neck skin to back with skewer. Fold wings across back with tips touching. Tuck drumsticks under band of skin at tail, or tie together with heavy kitchen string, then tie to tail.

3 In small bowl, combine 2 teaspoons dried sage, and the salt and pepper; rub into turkey skin. Place turkey, breast side up, on rack in shallow roasting pan. Brush with melted butter. Insert ovenproof meat thermometer so tip is in thickest part of inside thigh and does not touch bone.

4 Roast uncovered 3 to 4 hours. After about 2 hours of roasting, cut band of skin or string holding legs. Place tent of foil loosely over turkey when it begins to turn golden. Brush marmalade on turkey about 20 minutes before turkey is done. Thermometer will read 165°F when turkey is done, and drumsticks should move easily when lifted or twisted. Thermometer placed in center of stuffing will read 165°F when done.

5 Let stand about 15 minutes for easiest carving. Brush again with marmalade before carving.

1 Serving: Calories 930 (Calories from Fat 380); Total Fat 42g (Saturated Fat 15g; Trans Fat 1g); Cholesterol 325mg; Sodium 1010mg; Total Carbohydrate 39g (Dietary Fiber 2g); Protein 98g **% Daily Value:** Vitamin A 15%; Vitamin C 4%; Calcium 15%; Iron 25% **Exchanges:** 1½ Starch, 1 Other Carbohydrate, 13 Lean Meat, ½ Fat **Carbohydrate Choices:** 2½

To bake stuffing separately, place in greased 13x9-inch (3-quart) glass baking dish. Cover and bake at 325°F for 30 minutes; uncover and bake 5 minutes longer.

Mexicali Chicken-Tortilla Stew

Prep Time: 40 Minutes • Start to Finish: 40 Minutes • 5 servings (1½ cups each)

STEW

1 lb boneless skinless chicken breasts

1 carton (32 oz) Progresso® chicken broth

1 tablespoon olive oil

1 medium onion, chopped (½ cup)

2 teaspoons finely chopped garlic

1½ cups Old El Paso® Thick 'n Chunky salsa

1 cup Green Giant® Valley Fresh Steamers™ Niblets® frozen corn (from 12-oz bag)

1 tablespoon chili powder

4 soft corn tortillas (6 inch), cut into 1-inch pieces

1 can (14.5 oz) Muir Glen® diced fire-roasted tomatoes with garlic, undrained

1 can (15 oz) Progresso® black beans, drained, rinsed

TOPPING

⅓ cup gluten-free sour cream

¼ cup chopped fresh cilantro

1 In 3-quart saucepan, heat chicken and broth to boiling; reduce heat. Cover; simmer 20 minutes or until juice of chicken is clear when center of thickest part is cut (at least 165°F).

2 Meanwhile, in 4-quart Dutch oven, heat oil over medium heat. Cook onion and garlic in oil, stirring occasionally, until tender.

3 Remove chicken from broth; set aside. Add broth to Dutch oven. Stir in remaining stew ingredients. Cover; simmer 10 minutes. Shred or cut chicken into bite-size pieces; add to stew. Cook until thoroughly heated. Top individual servings with sour cream and cilantro.

1 Serving: Calories 440 (Calories from Fat 100); Total Fat 11g (Saturated Fat 3.5g; Trans Fat 0g); Cholesterol 65mg; Sodium 1600mg; Total Carbohydrate 50g (Dietary Fiber 12g); Protein 34g **% Daily Value:** Vitamin A 30%; Vitamin C 15%; Calcium 15%; Iron 25% **Exchanges:** 2½ Starch, 1 Other Carbohydrate, 3½ Lean Meat **Carbohydrate Choices:** 3

A can of great northern, pinto or navy beans would be just as delicious in this stew as the black beans. For those who prefer a spicier flavor, place a bottle of gluten-free red pepper sauce at the table and let people add the amount they like.

Chicken Noodle Soup

Prep Time: 30 Minutes • Start to Finish: 30 Minutes • 5 servings (1½ cups each)

1 tablespoon canola oil

2 boneless skinless chicken breasts (about ¾ lb), cut into ½-inch pieces

½ teaspoon gluten-free seasoned salt

½ teaspoon gluten-free garlic-pepper blend

1 medium onion, chopped (½ cup)

5½ cups Progresso® chicken broth (from two 32-oz cartons)

3 medium carrots, sliced (1½ cups)

1 medium stalk celery, sliced (½ cup)

1½ cups uncooked gluten-free quinoa rotelle pasta or other gluten-free spiral pasta (4 oz)

1 tablespoon chopped fresh or 1 teaspoon dried thyme leaves

1 In 4-quart saucepan, heat oil over medium-high heat. Cook chicken in oil 4 to 6 minutes, stirring occasionally, until no longer pink in center. Sprinkle chicken with seasoned salt and garlic-pepper blend. Add onion; cook 2 to 3 minutes, stirring occasionally, until tender.

2 Stir in broth, carrots and celery. Heat to boiling; reduce heat to medium. Cook 5 minutes.

3 Add pasta and thyme. Simmer uncovered 8 to 10 minutes, stirring occasionally, until pasta and vegetables are tender (do not overcook pasta).

1 Serving: Calories 290 (Calories from Fat 70); Total Fat 8g (Saturated Fat 1.5g; Trans Fat 0g); Cholesterol 40mg; Sodium 1350mg; Total Carbohydrate 31g (Dietary Fiber 1g); Protein 24g **% Daily Value:** Vitamin A 120%; Vitamin C 4%; Calcium 4%; Iron 10% **Exchanges:** 2 Starch, ½ Vegetable, 2½ Very Lean Meat, 1 Fat **Carbohydrate Choices:** 2

Gluten-free pasta is more fragile than regular pasta and will break apart, so be careful to not overcook it or stir it too much.

Chipotle Beef–Stuffed Peppers

Prep Time: 20 Minutes • Start to Finish: 1 Hour 10 Minutes • 4 servings

1 cup uncooked instant white rice

1 cup water

1 lb lean (at least 80%) ground beef

1 can (11 oz) Green Giant® Mexicorn® whole kernel corn with red and green peppers, drained

2 chipotle chiles in adobo sauce (from 7-oz can), chopped (2 tablespoons)

1 egg, beaten

1½ cups gluten-free shredded Monterey Jack cheese (6 oz)

4 medium red and/or green bell peppers

1 cup Old El Paso® Thick 'n Chunky salsa

¼ cup chopped green onions

1 Heat oven to 375°F. Cook rice in water as directed on package.

2 Meanwhile, in 12-inch nonstick skillet, cook beef over medium-high heat, stirring frequently, until thoroughly cooked; drain. Add corn, chiles and egg; mix well. Stir in cooked rice and 1 cup of the cheese.

3 Cut bell peppers in half lengthwise; remove seeds and membrane. Place cut side up in ungreased 13x9-inch (3-quart) glass baking dish. Spoon about ¾ cup beef mixture into each pepper half, mounding as necessary. Top each with 2 tablespoons salsa. Cover dish tightly with foil.

4 Bake 35 to 40 minutes or until peppers are crisp-tender. Uncover; sprinkle with remaining ½ cup cheese and the green onions. Bake uncovered 5 to 10 minutes longer or until cheese is melted.

1 Serving: Calories 610 (Calories from Fat 250); Total Fat 28g (Saturated Fat 13g; Trans Fat 1g); Cholesterol 160mg; Sodium 1360mg; Total Carbohydrate 52g (Dietary Fiber 4g); Protein 37g **% Daily Value:** Vitamin A 90%; Vitamin C 190%; Calcium 35%; Iron 25% **Exchanges:** 2 Starch, 1 Other Carbohydrate, 1 Vegetable, 4 Medium-Fat Meat, 1½ Fat **Carbohydrate Choices:** 3½

Chipotle chiles are simply dried jalapeños. You can purchase them dried in small bags or canned in a rich, spicy adobo sauce. In this recipe, we call for the canned variety to make use of the added flavor of the adobo sauce.

Impossibly Easy Chicken Club Pie

Prep Time: 10 Minutes • Start to Finish: 45 Minutes • 6 servings

1½ **cups diced cooked chicken**

¼ **cup diced cooked ham**

4 **slices gluten-free bacon, crisply cooked, crumbled**

1 **cup gluten-free shredded mozzarella cheese (4 oz)**

½ **cup Bisquick® Gluten Free mix**

1 **cup milk**

3 **eggs, beaten**

½ **cup gluten-free light Caesar dressing**

2 **cups shredded romaine lettuce**

1 **cup cherry tomatoes, cut in half**

1 Heat oven to 400°F. Spray 9-inch glass pie plate with cooking spray (without flour). In pie plate, layer chicken, ham, bacon and cheese.

2 In medium bowl, mix Bisquick mix, milk, eggs and ¼ cup of the dressing with whisk or fork until blended. Pour over ingredients in pie plate.

3 Bake 25 to 30 minutes or until knife inserted in center comes out clean. Let stand 5 minutes.

4 Meanwhile, in medium bowl, toss lettuce and tomatoes with remaining ¼ cup dressing. Cut pie into wedges; top each wedge with lettuce mixture.

1 Serving: Calories 280 (Calories from Fat 120); Total Fat 13g (Saturated Fat 5g; Trans Fat 0g); Cholesterol 160mg; Sodium 730mg; Total Carbohydrate 17g (Dietary Fiber 1g); Protein 25g **% Daily Value:** Vitamin A 40%; Vitamin C 6%; Calcium 25%; Iron 6% **Exchanges:** ½ Starch, ½ Other Carbohydrate, 3½ Very Lean Meat, 2 Fat **Carbohydrate Choices:** 1

Check ingredients on the labels of shredded cheese, a good source of calcium for strong bones, to be sure it's gluten-free.

Glazed Meat Loaf

Prep Time: 20 Minutes • Start to Finish: 1 Hour 40 Minutes • 6 servings (1 slice each)

MEAT LOAF

- 1½ lb lean (at least 80%) ground beef
- ½ cup finely crushed gluten-free cracker crumbs
- 2 tablespoons milk
- 2 tablespoons gluten-free ketchup
- 1 tablespoon gluten-free Dijon mustard
- 1 teaspoon dried sage leaves
- ½ teaspoon salt
- ¼ teaspoon pepper
- 1 small onion, finely chopped (⅓ cup)
- 1 egg

GLAZE

- ½ cup gluten-free ketchup
- 1 teaspoon gluten-free Dijon mustard
- 1 tablespoon packed brown sugar

1 Heat oven to 350°F. In large bowl, combine all meat loaf ingredients. Spread mixture in ungreased 8x4- or 9x5-inch loaf pan.

2 In small bowl, combine all glaze ingredients. Spread over meat loaf.

3 Bake uncovered 1 hour to 1 hour 15 minutes or until thermometer inserted in center of loaf reads 160°F. Drain. Let stand 5 minutes before slicing.

1 Serving: Calories 260 (Calories from Fat 130); Total Fat 14g (Saturated Fat 5g; Trans Fat 1g); Cholesterol 105mg; Sodium 640mg; Total Carbohydrate 13g (Dietary Fiber 0g); Protein 22g **% Daily Value:** Vitamin A 6%; Vitamin C 4%; Calcium 4%; Iron 15% **Exchanges:** 1 Starch, 2½ Medium-Fat Meat **Carbohydrate Choices:** 1

Instead of using the glaze, you can top the meat loaf with your favorite gluten-free barbecue sauce or just gluten-free ketchup.

To crush crackers, place a few crackers at a time in a plastic bag. Seal the bag, and crush crackers into fine crumbs with a rolling pin or the flat side of a meat mallet.

Sausage-Mushroom Lasagna

Prep Time: 35 Minutes • Start to Finish: 1 Hour 50 Minutes • 8 servings

1 **lb gluten-free bulk Italian pork sausage or ground beef**

1 **medium onion, chopped (½ cup)**

1 **package (8 oz) sliced fresh mushrooms (about 3 cups)**

1 **jar (25 oz) gluten-free spaghetti or marinara sauce**

1 **can (15 oz) gluten-free tomato sauce**

½ **cup water**

1½ **teaspoons dried basil leaves**

1 **container (15 oz) gluten-free ricotta cheese**

¼ **cup gluten-free grated Parmesan cheese**

2 **tablespoons chopped fresh parsley**

3 **cups gluten-free shredded mozzarella cheese (12 oz)**

12 **uncooked gluten-free lasagna noodles (from two 10-oz packages)**

1 In 4-quart Dutch oven, cook sausage, onion and mushrooms over medium heat, stirring occasionally, until sausage is no longer pink; drain. Stir in spaghetti sauce, tomato sauce, water and basil. In medium bowl, mix ricotta cheese, Parmesan cheese and parsley.

2 Heat oven to 350°F. In ungreased 13x9-inch (3-quart) glass baking dish, spread 1 cup of the meat sauce. Layer with 4 noodles, half of the ricotta mixture and one-third of the remaining meat sauce; sprinkle with 1 cup of the mozzarella cheese. Repeat with 4 more noodles, the remaining ricotta mixture, half of the remaining meat sauce and 1 cup mozzarella. Layer with remaining 4 noodles and meat sauce, making sure to cover noodles completely. Top with remaining mozzarella. Sprinkle with additional chopped fresh parsley, if desired.

3 Spray sheet of foil with cooking spray (without flour); place sprayed side down on lasagna. Bake 50 minutes. Uncover; bake 10 to 15 minutes longer or until hot and bubbly. Let stand 10 minutes before cutting.

1 Serving: Calories 560 (Calories from Fat 260); Total Fat 28g (Saturated Fat 12g; Trans Fat 0g); Cholesterol 65mg; Sodium 1120mg; Total Carbohydrate 46g (Dietary Fiber 3g); Protein 31g **% Daily Value:** Vitamin A 20%; Vitamin C 10%; Calcium 50%; Iron 15% **Exchanges:** 2 Starch, ½ Other Carbohydrate, 1 Vegetable, 3½ Medium-Fat Meat, 2 Fat **Carbohydrate Choices:** 3

You can prepare the lasagna the day before it's served; cover and refrigerate until ready to bake. Add about 5 to 10 minutes more baking time.

Beef Skillet Family Dinner

Prep Time: 30 Minutes • Start to Finish: 30 Minutes • 4 servings (1½ cups each)

1½ cups uncooked gluten-free quinoa rotelle pasta or other gluten-free spiral pasta (4 oz)

1 lb lean (at least 80%) ground beef

1 medium onion, chopped (½ cup)

½ teaspoon salt

¼ teaspoon pepper

1 can (14.5 oz) diced tomatoes with basil, garlic and oregano, undrained

1 can (8 oz) gluten-free tomato sauce

1 cup Green Giant® Valley Fresh Steamers™ Niblets® frozen corn (from 12-oz bag)

1½ teaspoons dried basil leaves

2 tablespoons chopped fresh parsley, if desired

1 Cook and drain pasta as directed on package.

2 Meanwhile, in 12-inch skillet, cook beef, onion, salt and pepper over medium-high heat 5 to 7 minutes, stirring occasionally, until beef is thoroughly cooked; drain.

3 Stir tomatoes, tomato sauce, corn and basil into skillet with beef. Heat to boiling, stirring occasionally. Reduce heat to low; simmer uncovered about 10 minutes, stirring occasionally, until tomatoes and corn are hot. Gently stir in cooked pasta. Sprinkle with parsley.

1 Serving: Calories 400 (Calories from Fat 130); Total Fat 14g (Saturated Fat 5g; Trans Fat 1g); Cholesterol 70mg; Sodium 800mg; Total Carbohydrate 43g (Dietary Fiber 2g); Protein 25g **% Daily Value:** Vitamin A 8%; Vitamin C 10%; Calcium 4%; Iron 20% **Exchanges:** 2½ Starch, 1 Vegetable, 2½ Medium-Fat Meat **Carbohydrate Choices:** 3

Be careful not to overcook the pasta or it will fall apart easily when stirred into the skillet.

You can use Italian seasoning for the dried basil, but be sure it's gluten-free.

Italian Hamburger Deep Dish

Prep Time: 15 Minutes • Start to Finish: 45 Minutes • 8 servings

1 lb lean (at least 80%) ground beef

2 teaspoons salt

⅛ teaspoon pepper

1 clove garlic, finely chopped

2⅔ cups water

¼ cup butter or margarine

2 tablespoons dried minced onion

1 teaspoon dried oregano leaves

⅔ cup milk

2⅔ cups Betty Crocker® Potato Buds® mashed potatoes

3 to 4 medium tomatoes, sliced

1 cup gluten-free shredded mozzarella cheese (4 oz)

1 Heat oven to 350°F. Grease 11x7x2-inch (2-quart) glass baking dish with shortening or cooking spray (without flour). In 10-inch skillet, cook beef, 1 teaspoon of the salt, the pepper and garlic over medium heat, stirring occasionally, until beef is browned; drain.

2 In 3-quart saucepan, heat water, butter, remaining 1 teaspoon salt, the onion and oregano to boiling. Remove from heat. Stir in milk and potatoes just until moistened. Let stand about 30 seconds or until liquid is absorbed; whip with fork until fluffy.

3 Spread half of the potato mixture in bottom of baking dish. Layer with beef and half of the tomatoes. Top with remaining potatoes and tomatoes. Sprinkle with cheese.

4 Bake uncovered about 30 minutes or until hot and bubbly.

1 Serving: Calories 350 (Calories from Fat 190); Total Fat 21g (Saturated Fat 11g; Trans Fat 1g); Cholesterol 75mg; Sodium 520mg; Total Carbohydrate 24g (Dietary Fiber 1g); Protein 17g **% Daily Value:** Vitamin A 15%; Vitamin C 6%; Calcium 15%; Iron 10% **Exchanges:** 1½ Starch, ½ Vegetable, 1½ Medium-Fat Meat, 2½ Fat **Carbohydrate Choices:** 1½

Change up this casserole with bulk gluten-free Italian sausage instead of ground beef.

Impossibly Easy Cheeseburger Pie

Prep Time: 15 Minutes • Start to Finish: 45 Minutes • 6 servings

1 **lb lean (at least 80%) ground beef**

1 **medium onion, chopped (½ cup)**

½ **teaspoon salt**

⅛ **teaspoon pepper**

1 **cup gluten-free shredded Cheddar cheese (4 oz)**

3 **eggs**

1 **cup milk**

½ **cup Bisquick® Gluten Free mix**

1 Heat oven to 400°F. Spray 9-inch glass pie plate with cooking spray (without flour). In 10-inch skillet, cook beef and onion over medium-high heat, stirring frequently, until beef is thoroughly cooked; drain. Stir in salt and pepper. Spread in pie plate; sprinkle with cheese.

2 In medium bowl, stir eggs, milk and Bisquick mix until blended. Pour into pie plate.

3 Bake 25 to 30 minutes or until knife inserted in center comes out clean.

1 Serving: Calories 310 (Calories from Fat 160); Total Fat 18g (Saturated Fat 9g; Trans Fat 1g); Cholesterol 175mg; Sodium 510mg; Total Carbohydrate 13g (Dietary Fiber 0g); Protein 23g **% Daily Value:** Vitamin A 8%; Vitamin C 0%; Calcium 20%; Iron 10% **Exchanges:** 1 Starch, 2½ Medium-Fat Meat, 1 Fat **Carbohydrate Choices:** 1

The milk and cheese in this easy dinner recipe are an excellent source of calcium, promoting strong bones and teeth.

Easy Sloppy Joe Pie

easy

Prep Time: 15 Minutes • Start to Finish: 45 Minutes • 6 servings

1 lb lean (at least 80%) ground beef

1 medium onion, chopped (½ cup)

1 can (15.5 oz) sloppy joe sauce

1 cup gluten-free shredded Cheddar cheese (4 oz)

2 eggs, slightly beaten

1 cup milk

1 cup Bisquick® Gluten Free mix

1 Heat oven to 400°F. Lightly grease bottom only of 8-inch square (2-quart) glass baking dish with shortening or cooking spray (without flour). In 10-inch skillet, cook beef and onion over medium heat, stirring occasionally, until beef is browned; drain. Stir in sloppy joe sauce and cheese. Spoon into baking dish.

2 In medium bowl, stir together remaining ingredients until blended. Pour over beef mixture.

3 Bake about 30 minutes or until golden brown.

1 Serving: Calories 400 (Calories from Fat 160); Total Fat 18g (Saturated Fat 8g; Trans Fat 1g); Cholesterol 140mg; Sodium 1330mg; Total Carbohydrate 38g (Dietary Fiber 3g); Protein 23g **% Daily Value:** Vitamin A 10%; Vitamin C 0%; Calcium 20%; Iron 15% **Exchanges:** 1 Starch, 1 Other Carbohydrate, ½ Low-Fat Milk, 2½ Lean Meat, 1½ Fat **Carbohydrate Choices:** 2½

Before baking, sprinkle with a tablespoon of sesame seed.

Cheesy Steak and Potato Skillet

Prep Time: 30 Minutes • Start to Finish: 30 Minutes • 4 servings

1 lb boneless beef sirloin steak, cut into 4 serving pieces

¾ teaspoon gluten-free seasoned salt

½ teaspoon gluten-free garlic-pepper blend

2 tablespoons butter or margarine

1½ cups frozen bell pepper and onion stir-fry (from 1-lb bag)

1 bag (20 oz) refrigerated home-style potato slices

1 cup gluten-free shredded American–Cheddar cheese blend (4 oz)

1 Sprinkle beef pieces with ¼ teaspoon of the seasoned salt and ¼ teaspoon of the garlic-pepper blend. In 12-inch nonstick skillet, cook beef over medium-high heat 3 to 4 minutes, turning once or twice, until brown and desired doneness. Remove from skillet; cover to keep warm.

2 In same skillet, melt butter over medium heat. Add stir-fry vegetables; cook 2 minutes, stirring frequently. Add potatoes; sprinkle with remaining ½ teaspoon seasoned salt and ¼ teaspoon garlic-pepper blend. Cook uncovered 8 to 10 minutes, stirring frequently, until tender.

3 Place beef in skillet with potatoes, pushing potatoes around beef. Cook 1 to 2 minutes, turning beef once, until hot. Sprinkle with cheese. Cover; heat until cheese is melted.

1 Serving: Calories 470 (Calories from Fat 170); Total Fat 19g (Saturated Fat 11g; Trans Fat 0.5g); Cholesterol 120mg; Sodium 700mg; Total Carbohydrate 33g (Dietary Fiber 2g); Protein 40g **% Daily Value:** Vitamin A 10%; Vitamin C 15%; Calcium 15%; Iron 20% **Exchanges:** 2 Starch, 1 Vegetable, 4½ Lean Meat, 1 Fat **Carbohydrate Choices:** 2

This easy skillet dish has everything going for it—it's high in iron and protein—yet still gluten-free.

Rosemary Pork Roast with Carrots

Prep Time: 15 Minutes • **Start to Finish:** 1 Hour 45 Minutes • 10 servings

Olive oil cooking spray

1 **boneless pork center loin roast (about 2½ lb)**

2 **teaspoons dried rosemary leaves, crushed**

1 **teaspoon salt**

¼ **teaspoon pepper**

2 **lb ready-to-eat baby-cut carrots**

1 **large sweet onion, cut into 16 wedges**

½ **teaspoon garlic powder**

1 Heat oven to 400°F. Spray 15x10x1-inch pan with olive oil cooking spray. Remove fat from pork. Spray pork with olive oil cooking spray; sprinkle with 1 teaspoon of the rosemary, ½ teaspoon of the salt and the pepper. Place in center of pan.

2 In large bowl, mix carrots, onion, garlic powder, the remaining teaspoon rosemary and ½ teaspoon salt. Arrange vegetable mixture around pork; spray vegetables with olive oil cooking spray.

3 Roast uncovered 1 hour to 1 hour 30 minutes or until meat thermometer inserted into center of pork reads 155°F and vegetables are tender. Remove from heat; cover with foil and let stand 10 minutes until thermometer reads 160°F. Slice pork; serve with vegetables.

1 Serving: Calories 240 (Calories from Fat 90); Total Fat 10g (Saturated Fat 3.5g; Trans Fat 0g); Cholesterol 70mg; Sodium 340mg; Total Carbohydrate 10g (Dietary Fiber 3g); Protein 26g **% Daily Value:** Vitamin A 310%; Vitamin C 6%; Calcium 4%; Iron 8% **Exchanges:** 2 Vegetable, 3 Lean Meat, ½ Fat **Carbohydrate Choices:** ½

Pork loin is a lean protein choice that provides structure to the body in skin, cell membranes and muscles.

Pork Chops and Apples

lowfat

Prep Time: 20 Minutes • **Start to Finish:** 1 Hour 5 Minutes • 2 servings

1   **medium unpeeled cooking apple, sliced**

2   **tablespoons packed brown sugar**

¼   **teaspoon ground cinnamon**

2   **pork rib chops, ½ to ¾ inch thick (about ¼ lb each)**

1 Heat oven to 350°F. Place apples in ungreased 1½-quart casserole. Sprinkle with brown sugar and cinnamon.

2 Remove fat from pork. Spray 8- or 10-inch skillet with cooking spray (without flour); heat over medium heat 1 to 2 minutes. Add pork; cook about 5 minutes, turning once, until light brown. Place pork in single layer on apples.

3 Cover; bake about 45 minutes or until pork is no longer pink in center and apples are tender.

1 Serving: Calories 200 (Calories from Fat 50); Total Fat 5g (Saturated Fat 2g; Trans Fat 0g); Cholesterol 45mg; Sodium 30mg; Total Carbohydrate 23g (Dietary Fiber 2g); Protein 15g **% Daily Value:** Vitamin A 0%; Vitamin C 2%; Calcium 2%; Iron 6% **Exchanges:** ½ Fruit, 1 Other Carbohydrate, 2 Lean Meat **Carbohydrate Choices:** 1½

Pork is a great source of thiamin, also called vitamin B$_1$. Thiamin is an important nutrient because it helps our bodies release energy in our gluten-free foods.

Basil Salmon and Julienne Vegetables

Prep Time: 15 Minutes • Start to Finish: 25 Minutes • 4 servings

1 teaspoon olive, canola or soybean oil

1 bag (1 lb) frozen bell pepper and onion stir-fry

1 medium zucchini, cut into julienne (matchstick-size) strips

1 salmon fillet (1 lb), cut into 4 pieces

2 tablespoons chopped fresh basil leaves

½ teaspoon gluten-free seasoned salt

1 teaspoon gluten-free lemon-pepper seasoning

¼ cup Progresso® chicken broth (from 32-oz carton)

1 Spray 12-inch skillet with cooking spray (without flour); add oil and heat over medium heat. Add bell pepper stir-fry; cook 2 minutes, stirring occasionally. Stir in zucchini.

2 Place salmon, skin side down, in skillet, pushing down into vegetables if necessary. Sprinkle salmon and vegetables with basil, seasoned salt and lemon-pepper seasoning. Pour broth over salmon and vegetables.

3 Reduce heat to medium-low; cover and cook 8 to 10 minutes or until salmon flakes easily with fork. Remove salmon and vegetables from skillet with slotted spoon.

1 Serving: Calories 210 (Calories from Fat 70); Total Fat 7g (Saturated Fat 2g; Trans Fat 0g); Cholesterol 65mg; Sodium 390mg; Total Carbohydrate 12g (Dietary Fiber 2g); Protein 23g **% Daily Value:** Vitamin A 8%; Vitamin C 40%; Calcium 4%; Iron 8% **Exchanges:** ½ Other Carbohydrate, 1 Vegetable, 3 Lean Meat **Carbohydrate Choices:** 1

Salmon is a super source of lean protein and vitamin B_3, niacin. Niacin helps our bodies release energy from the foods we eat.

Crunchy Ranch Fish Tacos

Prep Time: 35 Minutes • Start to Finish: 35 Minutes • 6 servings (2 tacos each)

1 box (4.6 oz) Old El Paso® taco shells (12 shells)

4 cups coleslaw mix (from 16-oz bag)

½ cup gluten-free ranch dressing

3 tablespoons chopped fresh cilantro

1 egg

1 tablespoon water

1 cup coarsely crushed gluten-free cracker crumbs (about 12 crackers)

¾ teaspoon salt

1 teaspoon chili powder

½ teaspoon ground red pepper (cayenne)

1 lb cod, tilapia or other medium-firm fish fillets

2 tablespoons canola oil

2 medium tomatoes, seeded, diced (about 2 cups)

1 Heat taco shells as directed on box. Meanwhile, in medium bowl, toss coleslaw, ranch dressing and cilantro; set aside.

2 In shallow dish, beat egg and water. In another shallow dish, mix cracker crumbs, salt, chili powder and red pepper. Dip fillets into egg mixture; coat well with crumb mixture.

3 In 12-inch nonstick skillet, heat oil over medium heat. Cook fillets in oil 6 to 8 minutes, turning once, until fish flakes easily with fork. Cut into bite-size pieces.

4 Fill warmed taco shells with fish, coleslaw mixture and tomatoes. Serve immediately.

1 Serving: Calories 370 (Calories from Fat 190); Total Fat 21g (Saturated Fat 4.5g; Trans Fat 0g); Cholesterol 80mg; Sodium 380mg; Total Carbohydrate 25g (Dietary Fiber 3g); Protein 18g **% Daily Value:** Vitamin A 35%; Vitamin C 25%; Calcium 6%; Iron 8% **Exchanges:** 1½ Starch, ½ Vegetable, 2 Lean Meat, 3 Fat **Carbohydrate Choices:** 1½

Serve the tacos with gluten-free refried beans or gluten-free Mexican-style rice.

Red Pepper and Broccoli Risotto

Prep Time: 55 Minutes • Start to Finish: 55 Minutes • 4 servings

2 teaspoons vegetable oil

1 large onion, chopped (1 cup)

4 cloves garlic, finely chopped

2 medium red bell peppers, chopped (2 cups)

2 cups sliced mushrooms (6 oz)

1½ cups uncooked Arborio or other short-grain rice

4¼ cups Progresso® chicken broth (from two 32-oz cartons)

2 cups broccoli florets

1 teaspoon salt

3 tablespoons gluten-free grated Parmesan cheese

⅓ cup chopped fresh parsley

1 In 12-inch nonstick skillet, heat oil over medium-high heat. Add onion, garlic, bell peppers and mushrooms; cook 3 to 5 minutes, stirring frequently, until onions are crisp-tender. Stir in rice. Cook 1 minute, stirring constantly.

2 Stir in ½ cup of the broth. Cook, stirring constantly, until liquid is completely absorbed. Stir in an additional ½ cup broth. Continue cooking about 20 minutes, adding broth ½ cup at a time after previous additions have been absorbed and stirring constantly, until rice is creamy and just tender; remove from heat. Stir in remaining ingredients. Let stand 1 minute.

1 Serving: Calories 420 (Calories from Fat 60); Total Fat 6g (Saturated Fat 2g; Trans Fat 0g); Cholesterol 0mg; Sodium 1790mg; Total Carbohydrate 75g (Dietary Fiber 4g); Protein 16g **% Daily Value:** Vitamin A 60%; Vitamin C 120%; Calcium 15%; Iron 25% **Exchanges:** 3½ Starch, ½ Other Carbohydrate, 3 Vegetable, 1 Fat **Carbohydrate Choices:** 5

Risotto is done when enough broth has been absorbed to make the rice just tender and the mixture creamy.

Vegetables, such as broccoli and red bell pepper, provide vitamins A, C and folic acid to this colorful gluten-free favorite.

Champagne Shrimp Risotto

Prep Time: 50 Minutes • Start to Finish: 50 Minutes • 6 servings

1 lb uncooked medium shrimp in shells, thawed if frozen

2 tablespoons butter or margarine

1 medium onion, thinly sliced

½ cup brut champagne, dry white wine or Progresso® chicken broth

1½ cups uncooked Arborio or other short-grain white rice

2 cups Progresso® chicken broth (from 32-oz carton), warmed

1 cup gluten-free clam juice or water, warmed

2 cups chopped arugula, watercress or spinach

⅓ cup gluten-free grated Parmesan cheese

½ teaspoon ground pepper

Chopped fresh parsley, if desired

1 Peel shrimp. Make a shallow cut lengthwise down back of each shrimp; wash out vein.

2 In 12-inch skillet or 4-quart Dutch oven, melt butter over medium-high heat. Add onion; cook, stirring frequently, until tender. Reduce heat to medium. Add shrimp; cook uncovered about 8 minutes, turning once, until shrimp are pink. Remove shrimp from skillet; keep warm.

3 Add champagne to onion in skillet; cook until liquid has evaporated. Stir in rice. Cook uncovered over medium heat about 5 minutes, stirring frequently, until edges of rice kernels are translucent. In 4-cup glass measuring cup, mix chicken broth and clam juice; pour ½ cup of the mixture over rice. Cook uncovered, stirring occasionally, until liquid is absorbed. Repeat with remaining broth mixture, ½ cup at a time, until rice is tender and creamy.

4 About 5 minutes before risotto is done, stir in shrimp, arugula, cheese and pepper. Sprinkle with parsley before serving.

1 Serving: Calories 320 (Calories from Fat 60); Total Fat 6g (Saturated Fat 3.5g; Trans Fat 0g); Cholesterol 125mg; Sodium 610mg; Total Carbohydrate 43g (Dietary Fiber 1g); Protein 19g **% Daily Value:** Vitamin A 8%; Vitamin C 4%; Calcium 10%; Iron 20% **Exchanges:** 2½ Starch, 1 Vegetable, 1½ Lean Meat **Carbohydrate Choices:** 3

Shrimp and rice create an excellent source of iron, a mineral important for transporting oxygen to working muscles.

Basil Penne with Asparagus and Feta

Prep Time: 35 Minutes • Start to Finish: 35 Minutes • 4 servings (1½ cups each)

2 cups uncooked gluten-free penne pasta (6 oz)

1 lb fresh asparagus, trimmed, cut diagonally into 1½-inch pieces

2 tablespoons olive oil

2 cloves garlic, finely chopped

1 can (15 oz) Progresso® cannellini beans, drained, rinsed

1½ cups halved grape or cherry tomatoes

¼ cup chopped fresh or 1 tablespoon dried basil leaves

2 tablespoons fresh lemon juice

½ teaspoon coarse sea salt

¼ teaspoon coarse ground black pepper

1 package (6 oz) gluten-free crumbled tomato-basil feta cheese

1 Cook and drain pasta as directed on package, adding asparagus during last 3 minutes of cooking time (don't overcook pasta).

2 Meanwhile, in 12-inch skillet, heat oil over medium heat. Cook garlic in oil about 3 minutes, stirring occasionally. Add beans, tomatoes, basil, lemon juice, salt and pepper; toss gently.

3 Stir cooked pasta and asparagus into skillet. Cook about 5 minutes, stirring occasionally, until thoroughly heated. Stir in cheese.

1 Serving: Calories 550 (Calories from Fat 170); Total Fat 19g (Saturated Fat 7g; Trans Fat 0g); Cholesterol 35mg; Sodium 810mg; Total Carbohydrate 70g (Dietary Fiber 11g); Protein 24g **% Daily Value:** Vitamin A 40%; Vitamin C 15%; Calcium 25%; Iron 40% **Exchanges:** 4 Starch, 2 Vegetable, 1 Lean Meat, 3 Fat **Carbohydrate Choices:** 4½

You can use any gluten-free pasta in this recipe and whatever beans you like or have on hand.

Chickpea and Tomato Curry

Prep Time: 30 Minutes • Start to Finish: 30 Minutes • 6 servings (1 cup each)

1 tablespoon olive or vegetable oil

1 medium onion, chopped (½ cup)

3 cloves garlic, finely chopped

1 tablespoon finely chopped gingerroot

1 tablespoon curry powder

2 cans (15 oz each) chickpeas, drained, rinsed

2 cans (14.5 oz each) Muir Glen® organic fire-roasted diced tomatoes, undrained

½ cup finely chopped fresh cilantro

1 tablespoon fresh lemon juice

½ teaspoon coarse (kosher or sea) salt

Hot cooked rice, if desired

Plain yogurt, if desired

1 In 3-quart saucepan, heat oil over medium heat. Add onion, garlic, gingerroot and curry powder; cook about 2 minutes, stirring frequently, until onion is tender.

2 Stir in chickpeas and tomatoes. Heat to boiling. Reduce heat; simmer uncovered 15 minutes, stirring occasionally. Stir in cilantro, lemon juice and salt.

3 Serve over rice. Top each serving with yogurt.

1 Serving: Calories 270 (Calories from Fat 50); Total Fat 6g (Saturated Fat 0.5g; Trans Fat 0g); Cholesterol 0mg; Sodium 380mg; Total Carbohydrate 42g (Dietary Fiber 10g); Protein 12g **% Daily Value:** Vitamin A 6%; Vitamin C 15%; Calcium 10%; Iron 30% **Exchanges:** 2 Starch, ½ Other Carbohydrate, 1 Vegetable, ½ Very Lean Meat, 1 Fat **Carbohydrate Choices:** 3

For the best flavor, look for cilantro that is very green, fresh looking and aromatic. This curry is nice served with basmati rice.

chapter 4

breads & sides

Gluten-Free Quick Bread Mix

Prep Time: 10 Minutes • Start to Finish: 10 Minutes • 6½ cups

1½ **cups white rice flour**

1½ **cups tapioca flour**

¾ **cup potato starch flour**

¾ **cup sweet white sorghum flour**

¾ **cup garbanzo and fava flour**

¾ **cup cornstarch**

3 **teaspoons xanthan gum**

3 **teaspoons gluten-free baking powder**

3 **teaspoons baking soda**

1½ **teaspoons salt**

1 In large bowl, mix all ingredients with whisk until fully incorporated. Spoon into large resealable freezer plastic bag. Store in freezer 6 to 9 months. Before using, shake bag thoroughly for several minutes to blend the flours and xanthan gum.

Contributed by Jean Duane Alternative Cook http://www.alternativecook.com

This simple mix makes enough to prepare Applesauce Quick Bread (page 132), Cinnamon Raisin Bread (page 131) and Gingerbread-Molasses Flax Muffins (page 133). Before placing the bag in the freezer, be sure to label it with the mix name and date. Having it on hand makes baking these treats a snap!

Cinnamon Raisin Bread

Prep Time: 15 Minutes • Start to Finish: 1 Hour 10 Minutes • 1 loaf (12 slices)

2 eggs

½ cup melted ghee or sunflower oil

½ cup almond milk, soymilk or regular milk

1½ teaspoons pure vanilla

½ cup packed brown sugar

¼ cup granulated sugar

2 cups Gluten-Free Quick Bread Mix (page 130)

2 teaspoons ground cinnamon

¾ cup raisins

1 Heat oven to 350°F. Spray 9x5-inch loaf pan with cooking spray (without flour).

2 In medium bowl, beat eggs, ghee, milk, vanilla, brown sugar and granulated sugar with electric mixer on medium speed until well blended. Add quick bread mix and cinnamon; beat about 1 minute until well blended. Stir in raisins. Pour batter into pan.

3 Bake 20 minutes. Cover loaf with cooking parchment paper; bake 25 minutes longer or until toothpick inserted in center comes out clean. Cool on cooling rack 10 minutes; remove from pan to cooling rack. Serve slightly warm.

1 Serving: Calories 250 (Calories from Fat 90); Total Fat 10g (Saturated Fat 6g; Trans Fat 0g); Cholesterol 55mg; Sodium 240mg; Total Carbohydrate 38g (Dietary Fiber 2g); Protein 2g **% Daily Value:** Vitamin A 6%; Vitamin C 0%; Calcium 6%; Iron 4% **Exchanges:** 1 Starch, 1½ Other Carbohydrate, 2 Fat **Carbohydrate Choices:** 2½

Contributed by Jean Duane Alternative Cook http://www.alternativecook.com

For variety, substitute any dried fruit, such as blueberries or strawberries, for the raisins.

For Cinnamon Raisin Muffins, divide batter evenly among 12 to 16 regular-size muffin cups sprayed with cooking spray (without flour). Decrease baking time to 25 minutes.

Applesauce Quick Bread

Prep Time: 15 Minutes • Start to Finish: 1 Hour 10 Minutes • 1 loaf (12 slices)

2 eggs

½ cup melted ghee or sunflower oil

½ cup applesauce

¼ cup Cascadian Farm® organic frozen (thawed) apple juice concentrate (from 12-oz can)

⅔ cup packed brown sugar

2 teaspoons pure vanilla

2 cups Gluten-Free Quick Bread Mix (page 130)

1 teaspoon ground cinnamon

1 Heat oven to 350°F. Spray 9x5-inch loaf pan with cooking spray (without flour).

2 In medium bowl, beat eggs, ghee, applesauce, apple juice concentrate, brown sugar and vanilla with electric mixer on medium speed until well blended. Add quick bread mix and cinnamon; beat about 1 minute until well blended. Pour batter into pan.

3 Bake 20 minutes. Cover loaf with cooking parchment paper; bake 25 minutes longer or until toothpick inserted in center comes out clean. Cool 10 minutes; remove from pan to cooling rack. Serve slightly warm.

1 Serving: Calories 270 (Calories from Fat 90); Total Fat 10g (Saturated Fat 6g; Trans Fat 0g); Cholesterol 55mg; Sodium 240mg; Total Carbohydrate 42g (Dietary Fiber 1g); Protein 2g **% Daily Value:** Vitamin A 6%; Vitamin C 0%; Calcium 4%; Iron 4% **Exchanges:** 1 Starch, 1½ Other Carbohydrate, 2 Fat **Carbohydrate Choices:** 3

Contributed by Jean Duane Alternative Cook http://www.alternativecook.com

Apple juice concentrate adds delicious flavor to this bread. For even more apple flavor, add ½ cup chopped dried apple bits to the batter; stir them in after beating in the quick bread mix and cinnamon.

The bread is covered with cooking parchment paper to prevent overbrowning. Look for cooking parchment paper with the foil, plastic wrap and waxed paper at the grocery store.

Gingerbread-Molasses Flax Muffins

Prep Time: 15 Minutes • Start to Finish: 50 Minutes • 16 muffins

2 eggs

½ cup sunflower or canola oil

¼ cup unsulphured molasses

½ cup almond milk, soymilk or regular milk

2 teaspoons pure vanilla

⅔ cup packed brown sugar

2 cups Gluten-Free Quick Bread Mix (page 130)

¼ cup ground flax meal

1 teaspoon ground ginger

1 Heat oven to 350°F. Spray 16 regular-size muffin cups with cooking spray (without flour).

2 In medium bowl, beat eggs, oil, molasses, milk, vanilla and brown sugar with electric mixer on medium speed until well blended. Add quick bread mix, flax meal and ginger; beat about 1 minute until well blended. Divide batter evenly among muffin cups, filling each about three-fourths full.

3 Bake 25 to 30 minutes or until toothpick inserted in center comes out clean. Cool 5 minutes; remove from pan to cooling rack. Serve warm.

1 Serving: Calories 190 (Calories from Fat 80); Total Fat 8g (Saturated Fat 1g; Trans Fat 0g); Cholesterol 25mg; Sodium 180mg; Total Carbohydrate 26g (Dietary Fiber 1g); Protein 2g **% Daily Value:** Vitamin A 0%; Vitamin C 0%; Calcium 6%; Iron 4% **Exchanges:** ½ Starch, 1 Other Carbohydrate, 1½ Fat **Carbohydrate Choices:** 2

Contributed by Jean Duane Alternative Cook http://www.alternativecook.com

> **Measure the oil first** and then the molasses in the same measuring cup. It will pour right out, and you'll have the right amount in your recipe every time.

Banana–Chocolate Chip Muffins

Prep Time: 20 Minutes • Start to Finish: 45 Minutes • 16 muffins

½ cup white rice flour

½ cup tapioca flour

½ cup potato starch flour

¼ cup sweet white sorghum flour

¼ cup garbanzo and fava flour

½ teaspoon xanthan gum

1 teaspoon gluten-free baking powder

1 teaspoon baking soda

½ teaspoon salt

2 eggs

½ cup sunflower or canola oil or melted ghee

¼ cup almond milk, soymilk or regular milk

1 cup mashed ripe bananas (2 medium)

⅔ cup packed brown sugar

2 teaspoons pure vanilla

½ cup miniature semisweet chocolate chips

1 Heat oven to 350°F. Spray 16 regular-size muffin cups with cooking spray (without flour).

2 In small bowl, mix flours, xanthan gum, baking powder, baking soda and salt with whisk; set aside. In medium bowl, beat eggs, oil, milk, bananas, brown sugar and vanilla with electric mixer on medium speed until well blended. Gradually add flour mixture, beating until well blended. Stir in chocolate chips. Divide batter evenly among muffin cups, filling each about three-fourths full.

3 Bake 18 to 20 minutes or until toothpick inserted in center comes out clean. Cool 5 minutes; remove from pan to cooling rack. Serve warm.

1 Serving: Calories 220 (Calories from Fat 80); Total Fat 9g (Saturated Fat 2g; Trans Fat 0g); Cholesterol 25mg; Sodium 200mg; Total Carbohydrate 30g (Dietary Fiber 2g); Protein 2g **% Daily Value:** Vitamin A 0%; Vitamin C 0%; Calcium 4%; Iron 4% **Exchanges:** 1 Starch, 1 Other Carbohydrate, 1½ Fat **Carbohydrate Choices:** 2

Contributed by Jean Duane Alternative Cook http://www.alternativecook.com

For Banana Date Muffins, substitute chopped dates (don't toss with flour) for the chocolate chips; add ½ cup chopped nuts and 1 teaspoon ground cinnamon.

This recipe is a great way to use bananas that are getting a little too ripe. You may find you buy bananas just to make these muffins!

Apple-Gingerbread Muffins

Prep Time: 20 Minutes • Start to Finish: 50 Minutes • 16 muffins

1 cup white rice flour

¼ cup sweet white sorghum flour

¼ cup tapioca flour

1 teaspoon xanthan gum

1½ teaspoons gluten-free baking powder

¾ teaspoon salt

2 teaspoons ground ginger

1 teaspoon ground cinnamon

¼ cup canola oil

2 eggs

3 tablespoons unsulphured molasses

¾ cup packed brown sugar

¼ cup water

1½ cups chopped peeled apple (about 1 large)

2 tablespoons gluten-free powdered sugar, if desired

1 Heat oven to 375°F. Place paper baking cup in each of 16 regular-size muffin cups.

2 In small bowl, mix flours, xanthan gum, baking powder, salt, ginger and cinnamon with whisk; set aside. In medium bowl, beat oil, eggs, molasses, brown sugar and water with electric mixer on medium speed until well blended. Gradually add flour mixture, beating on low speed just until combined. Stir in apple. Divide batter evenly among muffin cups.

3 Bake 20 to 25 minutes or until toothpick inserted in center comes out clean. Cool 5 minutes; remove from pan to cooling rack. Sprinkle powdered sugar over muffin tops. Serve warm.

1 Serving: Calories 150 (Calories from Fat 40); Total Fat 4.5g (Saturated Fat 0.5g; Trans Fat 0g); Cholesterol 25mg; Sodium 170mg; Total Carbohydrate 26g (Dietary Fiber 0g); Protein 1g **% Daily Value:** Vitamin A 0%; Vitamin C 0%; Calcium 4%; Iron 4% **Exchanges:** ½ Starch, 1 Other Carbohydrate, 1 Fat **Carbohydrate Choices:** 2

Contributed by Silvana Nardone Silvana's Kitchen http://silvanaskitchen.com

> If you can eat dairy, substitute ¼ cup melted butter for the oil.
>
> No sorghum flour in your pantry? Increase the white rice flour to 1¼ cups.

Lemon Blueberry Muffins

Prep Time: 15 Minutes • Start to Finish: 40 Minutes • 12 muffins

2 cups Bisquick® Gluten Free Mix

⅓ cup sugar

¾ cup milk

⅓ cup butter, melted

3 eggs, beaten

1 tablespoon grated lemon peel

1 cup fresh blueberries

2 tablespoons sugar

1 Heat oven to 400°F. Spray bottom only of 12 regular-size muffin cups with cooking spray (without flour), or place paper baking cup in each muffin cup.

2 In large bowl, stir Bisquick mix, ⅓ cup sugar, the milk, butter, eggs and lemon peel just until moistened. Fold in blueberries. Divide batter evenly among muffin cups. Sprinkle 2 tablespoons sugar evenly over muffins.

3 Bake 14 to 16 minutes or until set and lightly browned. Cool 5 minutes; remove from pan to cooling rack. Serve warm.

1 Serving: Calories 180 (Calories from Fat 60); Total Fat 7g (Saturated Fat 3.5g; Trans Fat 0g); Cholesterol 65mg; Sodium 280mg; Total Carbohydrate 27g (Dietary Fiber 1g); Protein 3g **% Daily Value:** Vitamin A 6%; Vitamin C 0%; Calcium 6%; Iron 0% **Exchanges:** ½ Starch, 1 Other Carbohydrate, 1½ Fat **Carbohydrate Choices:** 2

Sprinkle the muffin tops with coarse sugar instead of granulated sugar, if you like. You can use frozen blueberries instead of fresh—thaw completely and pat away excess moisture with a paper towel.

For Orange Blueberry Muffins, use 1 tablespoon grated orange peel for the lemon peel.

Apricot Muffins with Almond Streusel Topping

Prep Time: 25 Minutes • Start to Finish: 45 Minutes • 14 muffins

½ cup sorghum flour

½ cup tapioca flour

½ cup white rice flour

¼ cup garbanzo and fava flour

¼ cup potato starch flour

1 teaspoon gluten-free baking powder

1 teaspoon baking soda

1 teaspoon xanthan gum

½ teaspoon salt

2 eggs

1 cup gluten-free almond, rice, soy or regular milk

½ cup sunflower oil or melted ghee

½ cup granulated sugar

1 teaspoon apple cider vinegar

1 teaspoon pure vanilla

½ cup chopped dried apricots

TOPPING

¼ cup melted ghee

½ cup packed brown sugar

½ cup slivered almonds, toasted

1 Heat oven to 400°F. Place paper baking cup in each of 14 regular-size muffin cups; spray paper cups with cooking spray (without flour). In small bowl, stir together all flours, baking powder, baking soda, xanthan gum and salt; set aside.

2 In medium bowl, beat eggs, milk, oil, granulated sugar, vinegar and vanilla until well blended. Add flour mixture; stir until dry ingredients are moistened. Stir in apricots. Divide batter evenly among muffin cups, filling each until batter is ½ inch from top of paper baking cup.

3 In another small bowl, mix topping ingredients until crumbly. Sprinkle evenly over batter in cups.

4 Bake 25 to 30 minutes or until tops of muffins spring back when touched lightly in center. Cool 10 minutes. Remove muffins from pans; place on cooling racks. Carefully remove paper baking cups.

1 Muffin: Calories 300 (Calories from Fat 140); Total Fat 15g (Saturated Fat 4g; Trans Fat 0g); Cholesterol 40mg; Sodium 230mg; Total Carbohydrate 35g (Dietary Fiber 1g); Protein 3g **% Daily Value:** Vitamin A 8%; Vitamin C 0%; Calcium 6%; Iron 4% **Exchanges:** ½ Starch, 1 Fruit, 1 Other Carbohydrate, 3 Fat **Carbohydrate Choices:** 2

Contributed by Jean Duane Alternative Cook http://www.alternativecook.com

If you're substituting milk, try to find substitutes with the same fat content; unsweetened almond or hemp seed milk works beautifully in baked recipes as a dairy substitute. Both are available at natural grocery stores.

You can vary this recipe by substituting any dried fruit such as blueberries, cranberries or cherries.

Caramel Pecan Upside-Down Muffins

Prep Time: 15 Minutes • Start to Finish: 35 Minutes • 12 muffins

6 tablespoons plus ¼ cup butter or margarine, melted

¼ cup packed brown sugar

½ cup chopped pecans

1⅓ cups Bisquick® Gluten Free mix

⅓ cup granulated sugar

¼ cup butter, melted

½ cup milk

3 eggs, beaten

½ teaspoon ground cinnamon

1 Heat oven to 400°F. Spray 12 regular-size muffin cups with cooking spray (without flour).

2 In small bowl, mix 6 tablespoons butter, the brown sugar and pecans. Divide mixture evenly among muffin cups. In medium bowl, stir remaining ingredients until soft dough forms. Drop spoonfuls of dough into each muffin cup.

3 Bake 12 to 14 minutes or until toothpick inserted in center comes out clean. Turn pan upside down onto cookie sheet; leave pan over muffins 2 to 3 minutes to allow brown sugar mixture to drizzle over muffins. Remove pan; replace any topping left in pan on muffin tops. Serve warm.

1 Serving: Calories 230 (Calories from Fat 130); Total Fat 14g (Saturated Fat 7g; Trans Fat 0g); Cholesterol 80mg; Sodium 240mg; Total Carbohydrate 23g (Dietary Fiber 0g); Protein 3g **% Daily Value:** Vitamin A 8%; Vitamin C 0%; Calcium 4%; Iron 0% **Exchanges:** ½ Starch, 1 Other Carbohydrate, 3 Fat **Carbohydrate Choices:** 1½

For Caramel Almond Upside-Down Muffins, substitute sliced almonds for the pecans.

Serve with fresh fruit such as sliced cantaloupe, strawberries or pineapple chunks.

Strawberries-and-Cream Scones

Prep Time: 20 Minutes • Start to Finish: 50 Minutes • 10 scones

1 cup white rice flour

½ cup tapioca flour

¼ cup millet flour

¼ cup potato starch flour

2 teaspoons xanthan gum

3 tablespoons sugar

1 tablespoon gluten-free baking powder

½ teaspoon salt

6 tablespoons cold butter, cut into ¼-inch pieces

½ cup chopped fresh strawberries

1¼ cups whipping cream

1 Heat oven to 375°F. Line cookie sheet with cooking parchment paper.

2 In large bowl, mix flours, xanthan gum, 2 tablespoons sugar, the baking powder and salt with whisk. Cut in butter, using pastry blender (or pulling 2 table knives through ingredients in opposite directions), until coarse crumbs form. Add strawberries; stir gently to coat with crumb mixture. Stir in 1 cup plus 2 tablespoons whipping cream, mixing just until combined.

3 Onto cookie sheet, drop dough by ¼ cupfuls about 2 inches apart. Brush with remaining 2 tablespoons whipping cream; sprinkle with remaining 1 tablespoon sugar.

4 Bake 25 to 30 minutes or until golden and puffed. Remove to cooling rack. Serve warm.

1 Serving: Calories 280 (Calories from Fat 150); Total Fat 17g (Saturated Fat 10g; Trans Fat 0.5g); Cholesterol 50mg; Sodium 280mg; Total Carbohydrate 29g (Dietary Fiber 1g); Protein 2g **% Daily Value:** Vitamin A 10%; Vitamin C 4%; Calcium 10%; Iron 2% **Exchanges:** 1 Starch, 1 Other Carbohydrate, 3 Fat **Carbohydrate Choices:** 2

Contributed by Silvana Nardone Silvana's Kitchen http://silvanaskitchen.com

Use your family's favorite berries, such as raspberries or blueberries, in place of the strawberries.

If you can't find millet flour at your local supermarket, increase the white rice flour to 1¼ cups.

Cinnamon Scones

Prep Time: 10 Minutes • Start to Finish: 30 Minutes • 8 scones

SCONES

- 1 **cup potato starch flour**
- ⅔ **cup tapioca flour**
- ⅔ **cup white rice flour**
- 6 **tablespoons sugar**
- 4 **teaspoons gluten-free baking powder**
- 1 **teaspoon baking soda**
- 1 **teaspoon ground cinnamon**
- ½ **teaspoon salt**
- 2 **eggs**
- ⅔ **cup melted ghee or coconut oil**
- ¼ **cup gluten-free almond, rice, soy or cow's milk**
- 1 **teaspoon xanthan gum**
- 1 **teaspoon guar gum**

TOPPING

- 2 **tablespoons sugar**
- 1 **teaspoon cinnamon**

1 Heat oven to 400°F. Place nonstick baking mat or sheet of cooking parchment paper on cookie sheet; if using parchment paper, spray paper with cooking spray (without flour). In medium bowl, mix flours, 6 tablespoons sugar, the baking powder, baking soda, 1 teaspoon cinnamon and the salt.

2 In small bowl, beat eggs, melted ghee, milk and both gums with electric mixer until well blended. Add egg mixture to dry ingredients; beat with electric mixer on low speed until blended.

3 Coat work surface and hands with oil. Place dough on surface; pat into round, about 1 inch thick. Cut dough round into 8 wedges; place 1 inch apart on cookie sheet.

4 In small bowl, mix topping ingredients; sprinkle over dough.

5 Bake 14 to 18 minutes or until set. Remove from cookie sheet. Serve warm.

1 Scone: Calories 400 (Calories from Fat 180); Total Fat 20g (Saturated Fat 16g; Trans Fat 0g); Cholesterol 55mg; Sodium 570mg; Total Carbohydrate 54g (Dietary Fiber 1g); Protein 2g **% Daily Value:** Vitamin A 0%; Vitamin C 0%; Calcium 15%; Iron 2% **Exchanges:** 1½ Starch, 1 Fruit, 1 Other Carbohydrate, 3½ Fat **Carbohydrate Choices:** 3½

Contributed by Jean Duane Alternative Cook http://www.alternativecook.com

For Chocolate Scones, omit the cinnamon-sugar topping and stir ¼ cup miniature chocolate chips into the batter.

Using a drinking glass or round cutter, cut into rounds and use as shortcakes to serve with fresh chopped strawberries and whipped cream.

Blueberry Corn Muffins

Prep Time: 10 Minutes • Start to Finish: 30 Minutes • 18 muffins

1 box (15 oz) Betty Crocker® Gluten Free yellow cake mix

½ cup yellow cornmeal

¾ cup water

½ cup butter, melted

2 teaspoons pure vanilla

3 eggs, beaten

2 teaspoons grated orange peel

1½ cups fresh or frozen (unthawed) blueberries

1 tablespoon sugar

1 Heat oven to 375°F. Place paper baking cups in each of 18 regular-size muffin cups.

2 In large bowl, mix cake mix, cornmeal, water, butter, vanilla, eggs and orange peel just until dry ingredients are moistened. Gently stir in blueberries. Spoon evenly into muffin cups; sprinkle with sugar.

3 Bake 15 to 20 minutes or until toothpick inserted in center comes out clean. Immediately remove from pan. Serve warm or cool.

1 Muffin: Calories 170 (Calories from Fat 60); Total Fat 6g (Saturated Fat 3.5g; Trans Fat 0g); Cholesterol 50mg; Sodium 170mg; Total Carbohydrate 27g (Dietary Fiber 0g); Protein 2g **% Daily Value:** Vitamin A 4%; Vitamin C 0%; Calcium 0%; Iron 0% **Exchanges:** ½ Starch, 1½ Other Carbohydrate, 1 Fat **Carbohydrate Choices:** 2

These not-too-sweet muffins would be awesome with orange butter. Stir grated orange peel into softened butter and you've got it!

Doughnut Holes

Prep Time: 45 Minutes • Start to Finish: 45 Minutes • 24 doughnut holes

Vegetable oil

¼ cup granulated sugar

½ teaspoon ground cinnamon

1¼ cups Bisquick® Gluten Free mix

¼ cup packed brown sugar

¼ teaspoon ground nutmeg

2 tablespoons butter, melted

⅓ cup buttermilk

1 egg, beaten

1 In deep fryer or 2-quart heavy saucepan, heat 2 to 3 inches oil to 375°F. In shallow bowl, mix granulated sugar and cinnamon; set aside.

2 In medium bowl, mix remaining ingredients until smooth. Shape dough into 1¼-inch balls. Carefully drop balls, 5 or 6 at a time, into hot oil. Fry about 1 to 2 minutes or until golden brown on all sides; drain on paper towels. Immediately roll in cinnamon-sugar.

1 Serving: Calories 60 (Calories from Fat 20); Total Fat 2g (Saturated Fat 1g; Trans Fat 0g); Cholesterol 10mg; Sodium 85mg; Total Carbohydrate 10g (Dietary Fiber 0g); Protein 0g **% Daily Value:** Vitamin A 0%; Vitamin C 0%; Calcium 0%; Iron 0% **Exchanges:** ½ Starch, ½ Fat **Carbohydrate Choices:** ½

If you don't have buttermilk on hand, mix 1 teaspoon distilled white vinegar in ⅓ cup milk. Let stand 5 minutes and you have buttermilk!

Sandwich Bread

Prep Time: 30 Minutes • Start to Finish: 3 Hours 15 Minutes • 1 loaf (16 slices)

¾ cup warm water (105°F to 115°F)

1 tablespoon fast-rising dry yeast

¾ cup plus 1 tablespoon tapioca flour

½ cup white rice flour

¼ cup sorghum flour

¼ cup garbanzo and fava flour

½ cup plus 2 tablespoons potato starch flour

1½ teaspoons salt

1½ teaspoons gluten-free baking powder

1 teaspoon xanthan gum

2 eggs

¼ cup sugar

¼ cup sunflower oil

1 teaspoon guar gum

½ teaspoon apple cider vinegar

Cooking spray without flour

1 Spray bottom and sides of 8x4-inch loaf pan with cooking spray (without flour). In small bowl, mix water and yeast; set aside.

2 In another small bowl, stir together all flours, salt, baking powder and xanthan gum; set aside.

3 In medium bowl, beat remaining ingredients except cooking spray with electric mixer on medium speed 1 to 2 minutes. Beat in yeast mixture. Add flour mixture; beat on medium speed until thoroughly mixed. Pour into pan. Spray top of dough with cooking spray; if necessary, smooth top of dough with spatula. Cover with plastic wrap; let rise in warm place (80°F to 85°F) 1 hour to 1 hour 30 minutes or until dough rises to top of pan.

4 Heat oven to 375°F. Carefully remove plastic wrap from pan; bake 30 minutes. Reduce oven temperature to 350°F. Cover loaf with parchment paper; bake 25 to 30 minutes longer or until instant-read thermometer inserted in center of loaf reads 207°F. Cool on cooling rack 5 minutes. Remove loaf from pan; place on cooling rack. Cool completely, about 40 minutes.

1 Slice: Calories 120 (Calories from Fat 40); Total Fat 4.5g (Saturated Fat 0.5g; Trans Fat 0g); Cholesterol 25mg; Sodium 280mg; Total Carbohydrate 18g (Dietary Fiber 1g); Protein 2g **% Daily Value:** Vitamin A 0%; Vitamin C 0%; Calcium 4%; Iron 2% **Exchanges:** 1 Starch, 1 Fat **Carbohydrate Choices:** 1

Contributed by Jean Duane Alternative Cook http://www.alternativecook.com

Gluten-free bread looks "done" long before it is done, so don't be afraid to bake it for an hour.

Don't omit the xanthan gum! It's necessary to hold the bread together. Look for it in the gluten-free section of your grocery store or a natural foods store.

Sesame Seed Hamburger Buns

Prep Time: 25 Minutes • Start to Finish: 3 Hours 15 Minutes • 6 buns

1 tablespoon fast-rising dry yeast

¾ cup warm water (105°F to 115°F)

¾ cup plus 1 tablespoon tapioca flour

½ cup white rice flour

¼ cup sweet white sorghum flour

¼ cup garbanzo and fava flour

1½ teaspoons xanthan gum

1 teaspoon guar gum

½ cup plus 2 tablespoons cornstarch

1¾ teaspoons salt

1½ teaspoons gluten-free baking powder

2 eggs

⅓ cup sugar

¼ cup sunflower oil

½ teaspoon apple cider vinegar

1 tablespoon sesame seed

1 egg white, beaten

1 Line cookie sheet with cooking parchment paper; spray paper with cooking spray (without flour). In small bowl, dissolve yeast in warm water; set aside.

2 In medium bowl, mix flours, xanthan gum, guar gum, cornstarch, salt and baking powder with whisk; set aside. In large bowl, beat eggs, sugar, oil and vinegar with electric mixer on medium speed. Beat in yeast mixture. Gradually add flour mixture, beating on medium speed until well blended (dough will be sticky).

3 Using ¼-cup measure, drop dough into 6 portions onto cookie sheet. With wet hands, shape into buns, about 3¼x2 inches. Cover with plastic wrap; let rise in warm place about 1 hour 30 minutes or until doubled in size.

4 Heat oven to 350°F. Spread sesame seed in ungreased shallow pan. Bake uncovered 8 to 10 minutes, stirring occasionally, until golden brown. Set aside to cool. Remove plastic wrap from buns. Brush egg white over tops, being careful not to punch them down; sprinkle with toasted sesame seed.

5 Increase oven temperature to 375°F. Bake buns 15 minutes. Reduce oven temperature to 350°F. Cover buns with cooking parchment paper; bake 5 minutes longer or until instant-read thermometer inserted in center reads 207°F. Remove from cookie sheet to cooling rack; cool completely, about 1 hour. Split with serrated knife.

1 Bun: Calories 400 (Calories from Fat 110); Total Fat 13g (Saturated Fat 1.5g; Trans Fat 0g); Cholesterol 70mg; Sodium 850mg; Total Carbohydrate 66g (Dietary Fiber 3g); Protein 6g **% Daily Value:** Vitamin A 0%; Vitamin C 0%; Calcium 8%; Iron 6% **Exchanges:** 2½ Starch, 2 Other Carbohydrate, 2 Fat **Carbohydrate Choices:** 4½

Contributed by Jean Duane Alternative Cook http://www.alternativecook.com

Gluten-free bread dough is more like a batter and is very sticky. The floured surface commonly used with gluten-containing dough doesn't work with this type of dough. For best results, use wet hands to work with it and shape it.

Cornbread

easy

Prep Time: 10 Minutes • Start to Finish: 35 Minutes • 9 servings

¾ **cup cornmeal**

½ **cup tapioca flour**

¼ **cup white rice flour**

¼ **cup sorghum flour**

¼ **cup potato starch flour**

2 **teaspoons gluten-free baking powder**

1 **teaspoon baking soda**

1 **teaspoon salt**

½ **teaspoon xanthan gum**

½ **teaspoon guar gum**

1¼ **cups gluten-free almond, rice, soy or regular milk**

1 **teaspoon apple cider vinegar**

⅓ **cup sugar**

2 **eggs**

¼ **cup melted ghee**

1 Heat oven to 400°F. Spray bottom and sides of 8-inch square (2-quart) glass baking dish with cooking spray (without flour).

2 In medium bowl, stir together cornmeal, all flours, baking powder, baking soda, salt and both gums; set aside.

3 In medium bowl, beat milk, vinegar, sugar and eggs with electric mixer on medium speed until frothy. Gradually add ghee, beating continuously until thoroughly mixed. Add cornmeal mixture; beat on low speed about 1 minute or until well blended. Pour into baking dish.

4 Bake 20 to 25 minutes or until top springs back when touched lightly in center and cornbread pulls away from sides of baking dish. Cool 15 minutes. Serve warm.

1 Serving: Calories 240 (Calories from Fat 80); Total Fat 9g (Saturated Fat 5g; Trans Fat 0g); Cholesterol 60mg; Sodium 540mg; Total Carbohydrate 37g (Dietary Fiber 1g); Protein 4g **% Daily Value:** Vitamin A 8%; Vitamin C 0%; Calcium 10%; Iron 6% **Exchanges:** 1½ Starch, 1 Other Carbohydrate, 1½ Fat **Carbohydrate Choices:** 2½

Contributed by Jean Duane Alternative Cook http://www.alternativecook.com

Ghee is clarified butter; it adds a buttery taste and is measured when melted. Just microwave it on High for a minute or two to melt it. If you'd prefer, substitute sunflower or corn oil for the ghee in this recipe.

Dinner Rolls

Prep Time: 30 Minutes • Start to Finish: 2 Hours 15 Minutes • 24 rolls

½ cup warm water (105°F to 115°F)

1 teaspoon unflavored gelatin

2¼ teaspoons fast-rising dry yeast

½ cup sorghum flour

½ cup brown rice flour

½ cup white rice flour

⅓ cup tapioca flour

⅓ cup garbanzo and fava flour

¾ cup potato starch flour

¾ cup cornstarch

2 eggs

½ cup gluten-free almond, rice, soy or regular milk

¼ cup honey

3 tablespoons sunflower oil or melted ghee

1 teaspoon apple cider vinegar

2 teaspoons xanthan gum

1½ teaspoons salt

1 Spray 24 regular-size muffin cups with cooking spray (without flour). In small bowl, mix water, gelatin and yeast; set aside. In medium bowl, stir together all flours, and the cornstarch; set aside.

2 In food processor, place eggs, milk, honey, oil, vinegar, xanthan gum and salt. Process about 30 seconds or until well blended. Add flour mixture and yeast mixture; process about 30 seconds or until well blended.

3 Spray 2 teaspoons with cooking spray (without flour). Spoon 3 balls of dough into each muffin cup, re-spraying spoons as necessary. Spray sheet of plastic wrap with cooking spray (without flour); cover dough in pans. Let rise in warm place (80°F to 85°F) 1 hour to 1 hour 30 minutes or until doubled in size.

4 Heat oven to 375°F. Bake 14 to 16 minutes or until light golden brown. Immediately turn rolls out of pans onto cooling racks. Serve warm.

1 Roll: Calories 120 (Calories from Fat 25); Total Fat 2.5g (Saturated Fat 0g; Trans Fat 0g); Cholesterol 20mg; Sodium 160mg; Total Carbohydrate 22g (Dietary Fiber 1g); Protein 2g **% Daily Value:** Vitamin A 0%; Vitamin C 0%; Calcium 0%; Iron 2% **Exchanges:** 1½ Starch **Carbohydrate Choices:** 1½

Contributed by Jean Duane Alternative Cook http://www.alternativecook.com

> **Although** these are fantastic right out of the oven, they can also be baked and frozen in an airtight container, then popped into the toaster oven when you're ready to serve them.

Cheese-Garlic Biscuits

Prep Time: 5 Minutes • Start to Finish: 15 Minutes • 10 biscuits

BISCUITS

- **2 cups Bisquick® Gluten Free mix**
- **¼ teaspoon garlic powder**
- **¼ cup cold butter or margarine**
- **⅔ cup milk**
- **½ cup gluten-free shredded Cheddar cheese (2 oz)**
- **3 eggs**

GARLIC-BUTTER TOPPING

- **¼ cup butter or margarine, melted**
- **¼ teaspoon garlic powder**

1 Heat oven to 425°F. In medium bowl, stir together Bisquick mix and ¼ teaspoon garlic powder. Using pastry blender or fork, cut in ¼ cup cold butter until mixture looks like coarse crumbs. Stir in milk, cheese and eggs until soft dough forms.

2 Drop dough by 10 spoonfuls onto ungreased cookie sheet.

3 Bake 8 to 10 minutes or until light golden brown. In small bowl, mix ¼ cup melted butter and ¼ teaspoon garlic powder; brush on warm biscuits before removing from cookie sheet. Serve warm.

1 Biscuit: Calories 230 (Calories from Fat 120); Total Fat 13g (Saturated Fat 8g; Trans Fat 0g); Cholesterol 95mg; Sodium 400mg; Total Carbohydrate 22g (Dietary Fiber 0g); Protein 5g **% Daily Value:** Vitamin A 10%; Vitamin C 0%; Calcium 10%; Iron 0% **Exchanges:** 1½ Starch, 2½ Fat **Carbohydrate Choices:** 1½

Add about 1 tablespoon finely chopped fresh parsley to the Bisquick mix and garlic powder to add a little color to these biscuits.

Best-Ever Banana Bread

Prep Time: 10 Minutes • Start to Finish: 2 Hours • 1 loaf (16 slices)

½ cup tapioca flour

½ cup white rice flour

¼ cup garbanzo and fava flour

¼ cup sorghum flour

½ cup potato starch flour

1 teaspoon xanthan gum

½ teaspoon guar gum

1 teaspoon gluten-free baking powder

1 teaspoon baking soda

1 teaspoon ground cinnamon

1 teaspoon salt

¾ cup packed brown sugar

1 cup mashed very ripe bananas (2 medium)

½ cup melted ghee

¼ cup gluten-free almond, rice, soy or regular milk

1 teaspoon pure vanilla

2 eggs

1 Heat oven to 350°F. Generously spray bottom and sides of 9x5-inch loaf pan with cooking spray (without flour). In small bowl, stir together all flours, both gums, baking powder, baking soda, cinnamon and salt; set aside.

2 In medium bowl, beat remaining ingredients with whisk until blended. Add flour mixture; stir until thoroughly mixed. Pour into pan.

3 Bake 30 minutes. Cover with foil; bake 25 to 30 minutes or until toothpick inserted in center comes out almost clean. Cool 5 minutes. Remove loaf from pan; place on cooling rack. Cool completely, about 1 hour. Wrap tightly and store in refrigerator.

1 Slice: Calories 200 (Calories from Fat 80); Total Fat 9g (Saturated Fat 5g; Trans Fat 0g); Cholesterol 40mg; Sodium 270mg; Total Carbohydrate 29g (Dietary Fiber 1g); Protein 2g **% Daily Value:** Vitamin A 6%; Vitamin C 0%; Calcium 4%; Iron 2% **Exchanges:** 1 Starch, ½ Fruit, ½ Other Carbohydrate, 1½ Fat **Carbohydrate Choices:** 2

Contributed by Jean Duane Alternative Cook http://www.alternativecook.com

To make Apple Bread, substitute applesauce for the mashed bananas.

To make Pumpkin Bread, substitute canned pumpkin (not pumpkin pie mix) for the mashed bananas and add ¼ teaspoon ground cloves and ¼ teaspoon ground nutmeg.

Combining flours, starches and gums makes a great-tasting gluten-free bread.

Banana Nut Bread

Prep Time: 10 Minutes • **Start to Finish:** 2 Hours 5 Minutes • 1 loaf (14 slices)

½ **cup butter, softened**

1 **cup sugar**

1 **cup mashed ripe bananas (2 medium)**

2 **eggs, beaten**

2½ **cups Bisquick® Gluten Free mix**

½ **teaspoon ground cinnamon**

¼ **teaspoon ground cloves**

½ **cup buttermilk**

½ **cup chopped walnuts**

1 Heat oven to 350°F. Spray bottom only of 9x5-inch loaf pan with cooking spray (without flour).

2 In large bowl, beat butter and sugar with electric mixer on medium speed 2 minutes. Beat in bananas and eggs until well blended. On low speed, beat in Bisquick mix, cinnamon, cloves and buttermilk. Stir in nuts. Pour into pan.

3 Bake 1 hour to 1 hour 10 minutes or until toothpick inserted in center comes out clean. Cool 10 minutes. Run knife around edge of pan to loosen loaf; remove from pan to cooling rack. Cool completely, about 45 minutes.

1 Serving: Calories 260 (Calories from Fat 100); Total Fat 11g (Saturated Fat 5g; Trans Fat 0g); Cholesterol 50mg; Sodium 310mg; Total Carbohydrate 38g (Dietary Fiber 1g); Protein 3g **% Daily Value:** Vitamin A 6%; Vitamin C 0%; Calcium 6%; Iron 0% **Exchanges:** 1½ Starch, 1 Other Carbohydrate, 2 Fat **Carbohydrate Choices:** 2½

Flavored butter would be delicious with this banana bread. Try mixing ¼ cup softened butter with ¼ teaspoon grated orange peel.

Glazed Lemon–Pecan Bread

Prep Time: 15 Minutes • Start to Finish: 45 Minutes • 1 loaf (12 slices)

BREAD

- ½ **cup white rice flour**
- ½ **cup tapioca flour**
- ½ **cup potato starch flour**
- ¼ **cup sweet white sorghum flour**
- ¼ **cup garbanzo and fava flour**
- 1 **teaspoon xanthan gum**
- 1 **teaspoon gluten-free baking powder**
- 1 **teaspoon baking soda**
- ½ **teaspoon salt**
- 2 **eggs**
- ½ **cup sunflower or canola oil or melted ghee**
- ¼ **cup almond milk, soymilk or regular milk**
- ½ **teaspoon apple cider vinegar**
- 1 **tablespoon grated lemon peel**
- ¼ **cup fresh lemon juice**
- ⅔ **cup granulated sugar**
- ½ **cup chopped pecans**

GLAZE

- 2 **tablespoons fresh lemon juice**
- 1 **cup gluten-free powdered sugar**

1 Heat oven to 350°F. Spray 9x5-inch loaf pan with cooking spray (without flour).

2 In small bowl, mix flours, xanthan gum, baking powder, baking soda and salt with whisk; set aside. In medium bowl, beat eggs, oil, milk, vinegar, lemon peel, ¼ cup lemon juice and the granulated sugar with electric mixer on medium speed until well blended. Gradually add flour mixture, beating until well blended. Stir in pecans. Pour batter into pan.

3 Bake 20 minutes. Cover loaf with cooking parchment paper; bake 25 minutes longer or until golden brown. Cool 10 minutes; remove from pan to cooling rack.

4 In small bowl, stir glaze ingredients until smooth. With fork, poke holes in top of loaf; drizzle glaze over loaf. Serve slightly warm.

1 Serving: Calories 300 (Calories from Fat 120); Total Fat 14g (Saturated Fat 1.5g; Trans Fat 0g); Cholesterol 35mg; Sodium 260mg; Total Carbohydrate 41g (Dietary Fiber 2g); Protein 3g **% Daily Value:** Vitamin A 0%; Vitamin C 4%; Calcium 4%; Iron 4% **Exchanges:** 1 Starch, 1½ Other Carbohydrate, 2½ Fat **Carbohydrate Choices:** 3

Contributed by Jean Duane Alternative Cook http://www.alternativecook.com

A zester makes grating lemons a breeze. Just go as deep as the outer skin, avoiding the pith (the bitter white part of the skin). When you are ready to juice the lemon, roll it on the countertop before cutting it open. This releases the juice.

Soft Pretzels

Prep Time: 30 Minutes • Start to Finish: 2 Hours 15 Minutes • 12 pretzels

PRETZELS

4½ teaspoons regular active dry yeast

⅔ cup warm water (105°F to 115°F)

1 cup tapioca flour

⅔ cup sweet white sorghum flour

¼ cup garbanzo and fava flour

1 cup cornstarch

1½ teaspoons xanthan gum

½ teaspoon guar gum

1 teaspoon salt

3 eggs

1 tablespoon sugar

1 tablespoon honey

Additional garbanzo and fava flour

SODA BATH

Cooking spray (without flour)

⅔ cup baking soda

10 cups water

TOPPING

1 egg, beaten

1 tablespoon kosher (coarse) salt

1 Line cookie sheet with cooking parchment paper; spray paper with cooking spray (without flour). In small bowl, dissolve yeast in warm water; set aside.

2 In small bowl, mix flours, cornstarch, xanthan gum, guar gum and 1 teaspoon salt with whisk; set aside. In medium bowl, beat 3 eggs, the sugar and honey with electric mixer on medium speed 1 minute or until well blended. Add yeast mixture and flour mixture; beat 1 minute or until blended.

3 Divide dough into 12 equal-size balls. On work surface sprinkled with additional garbanzo and fava flour, roll each ball into 13x¾-inch rope. Carefully place ropes on cookie sheet; form into U shape and twist in middle. Spray tops of pretzels with cooking spray (without flour). Cover with plastic wrap; let rise in warm place 1 hour to 1 hour 30 minutes or until doubled in size.

4 Heat oven to 375°F. In 4-quart saucepan or Dutch oven, stir baking soda into water until dissolved. Heat to full rolling boil. Carefully place 1 pretzel at a time in water; boil 25 seconds. Remove with slotted spoon and return to cookie sheet. Brush tops of pretzels with egg, being careful not to fill openings with egg; sprinkle with kosher salt.

5 Bake 12 to 15 minutes or until golden brown. Immediately remove from cookie sheet to cooling rack.

1 Pretzel: Calories 160 (Calories from Fat 20); Total Fat 2g (Saturated Fat 0.5g; Trans Fat 0g); Cholesterol 70mg; Sodium 4140mg; Total Carbohydrate 30g (Dietary Fiber 2g); Protein 4g **% Daily Value:** Vitamin A 0%; Vitamin C 0%; Calcium 0%; Iron 4% **Exchanges:** 2 Starch **Carbohydrate Choices:** 2

Contributed by Jean Duane Alternative Cook http://www.alternativecook.com

Place cooled pretzels individually in resealable food-storage plastic sandwich bags. Place those bags in gallon-size freezer plastic bag and store in the freezer. For a quick snack anytime, take a pretzel out of the freezer and reheat in a toaster oven about 5 to 7 minutes.

Garden-Fresh Greek Salad

Prep Time: 20 Minutes • Start to Finish: 20 Minutes • 6 servings (1⅓ cups each)

GREEK DRESSING

- 3 tablespoons fresh lemon juice
- 1 tablespoon chopped fresh or 1 teaspoon dried oregano leaves
- ½ teaspoon salt
- ½ teaspoon sugar
- ½ teaspoon Dijon mustard
- ¼ teaspoon pepper
- 1 clove garlic, finely chopped

SALAD

- 1 bag (10 oz) ready-to-eat romaine lettuce
- ¾ cup chopped seeded peeled cucumber
- ½ cup sliced red onion
- ¼ cup sliced kalamata olives
- 2 medium tomatoes, seeded, chopped (1½ cups)
- ¼ cup reduced-fat feta cheese

1 In small bowl, beat all dressing ingredients with whisk.

2 In large bowl, toss all salad ingredients except cheese. Stir in dressing until salad is well coated. Sprinkle with cheese.

1 Serving: Calories 45 (Calories from Fat 15); Total Fat 1.5g (Saturated Fat 0.5g; Trans Fat 0g); Cholesterol 0mg; Sodium 340mg; Total Carbohydrate 6g (Dietary Fiber 2g); Protein 3g **% Daily Value:** Vitamin A 30%; Vitamin C 40%; Calcium 6%; Iron 6% **Exchanges:** 1 Vegetable, ½ Fat **Carbohydrate Choices:** ½

Feta cheese is often made from cow's milk, although traditionally it is made from sheep or goat's milk.

Broccoli and Squash Medley

Prep Time: 30 Minutes • Start to Finish: 30 Minutes • 14 servings (½ cup each)

2 bags (12 oz each) Green Giant® Valley Fresh Steamers™ frozen broccoli cuts

2 cups cubed (½ inch) peeled butternut squash (1½ lb)

½ cup orange juice

¼ cup butter or margarine, melted

½ cup sweetened dried cranberries

½ cup finely chopped pecans, toasted

1 tablespoon grated orange peel

1 teaspoon salt

1 Cook broccoli as directed on bag; set aside.

2 Meanwhile, in 12-inch skillet, cook squash in orange juice over medium-low heat 8 to 10 minutes, stirring frequently, until tender but firm.

3 Stir in butter, broccoli, cranberries, pecans, orange peel and salt; toss to coat. Serve immediately.

1 Serving: Calories 110 (Calories from Fat 60); Total Fat 6g (Saturated Fat 2.5g; Trans Fat 0g); Cholesterol 10mg; Sodium 210mg; Total Carbohydrate 12g (Dietary Fiber 2g); Protein 2g **% Daily Value:** Vitamin A 110%; Vitamin C 25%; Calcium 4%; Iron 4% **Exchanges:** 1 Starch, 1 Fat **Carbohydrate Choices:** 1

Vitamins A and C abound in this rainbow-hued side dish. Go ahead and personalize it—use your favorite nut and vary the cranberries with raisins, golden raisins or even chopped dried apricots.

Green Beans with Lemon-Herb Butter

Prep Time: 10 Minutes • Start to Finish: 20 Minutes • 4 servings

1 **bag (12 oz) Green Giant® Valley Fresh Steamers™ green beans**

3 **tablespoons butter (do not use margarine)**

1 **teaspoon grated lemon peel**

1 **teaspoon dried marjoram leaves**

¼ **teaspoon salt**

Lemon slices, if desired

1 Cook green beans as directed on bag; drain.

2 Meanwhile, in 2-quart saucepan, heat butter over medium heat until melted and beginning to brown; immediately remove from heat. Stir in lemon peel, marjoram and salt.

3 Pour butter mixture over beans; toss to coat. Garnish with lemon slices.

1 Serving: Calories 100 (Calories from Fat 80); Total Fat 9g (Saturated Fat 4.5g; Trans Fat 0.5g); Cholesterol 25mg; Sodium 210mg; Total Carbohydrate 5g (Dietary Fiber 2g); Protein 1g **% Daily Value:** Vitamin A 15%; Vitamin C 4%; Calcium 4%; Iron 4% **Exchanges:** 1 Vegetable, 2 Fat **Carbohydrate Choices:** ½

Be sure to use real butter in this recipe. The toasty flavor that comes from browning is possible only with butter, not margarine.

Veggies and Kasha with Balsamic Vinaigrette easy

Prep Time: 15 Minutes • Start to Finish: 1 Hour 15 Minutes • 4 servings (1 cup each)

SALAD

- 1 **cup water**
- ½ **cup uncooked buckwheat kernels (kasha)**
- 4 **medium green onions, thinly sliced (¼ cup)**
- 2 **medium tomatoes, seeded, coarsely chopped (1½ cups)**
- 1 **medium unpeeled cucumber, seeded, chopped (1¼ cups)**

VINAIGRETTE

- 2 **tablespoons balsamic or red wine vinegar**
- 1 **tablespoon olive oil**
- 2 **teaspoons sugar**
- ½ **teaspoon salt**
- ¼ **teaspoon pepper**
- 1 **clove garlic, finely chopped**

1 In 8-inch skillet, heat water to boiling. Add kasha; cook over medium-high heat 7 to 8 minutes, stirring occasionally, until tender. Drain if necessary.

2 In large bowl, mix kasha and remaining salad ingredients.

3 In tightly covered container, shake all vinaigrette ingredients until blended. Pour vinaigrette over kasha mixture; toss. Cover; refrigerate 1 to 2 hours to blend flavors.

1 Serving: Calories 120 (Calories from Fat 35); Total Fat 4g (Saturated Fat 0.5g; Trans Fat 0g); Cholesterol 0mg; Sodium 300mg; Total Carbohydrate 18g (Dietary Fiber 3g); Protein 3g **% Daily Value:** Vitamin A 15%; Vitamin C 20%; Calcium 2%; Iron 4% **Exchanges:** ½ Starch, ½ Other Carbohydrate, 1 Vegetable, ½ Fat **Carbohydrate Choices:** 1

Kasha, made from buckwheat, is gluten-free despite having "wheat" in its name—plus it offers a half serving of whole grain benefits.

Baked Potato Wedges

Prep Time: 15 Minutes • Start to Finish: 45 Minutes • 4 servings

¾ teaspoon salt

½ teaspoon sugar

½ teaspoon paprika

¼ teaspoon ground mustard

¼ teaspoon garlic powder, if desired

3 large baking potatoes (russet or Idaho), about 8 oz each

Cooking spray (without flour)

1 Heat the oven to 425°F. In small bowl or measuring cup, mix salt, sugar, paprika, mustard and garlic powder.

2 Cut each potato in half lengthwise. Turn potatoes cut sides down, and cut each half lengthwise into 4 wedges. In 13x9-inch pan, arrange potato wedges with skin sides down.

3 Spray potato wedges with cooking spray (without flour) until lightly coated. Sprinkle with salt mixture.

4 Bake uncovered 25 to 30 minutes or until potatoes are tender when pierced with a fork. Baking time will vary depending on size and type of potatoes used.

1 Serving: Calories 140 (Calories from Fat 10); Total Fat 1g (Saturated Fat 0g; Trans Fat 0g); Cholesterol 0mg; Sodium 460mg; Total Carbohydrate 28g (Dietary Fiber 3g); Protein 3g **% Daily Value:** Vitamin A 4%; Vitamin C 10%; Calcium 2%; Iron 8% **Exchanges:** 1½ Starch **Carbohydrate Choices:** 2

Cut potatoes into wedges just before using, or the cut sides will turn brown. Use russet or Idaho potatoes because they are best for baking.

Caramelized-Onion and Sweet Potato Skillet

Prep Time: 10 Minutes • Start to Finish: 30 Minutes • 4 servings

1 teaspoon vegetable oil

¼ large sweet onion (Bermuda, Maui or Spanish), sliced

3 medium sweet potatoes, peeled and sliced (3½ cups)

2 tablespoons packed brown sugar

½ teaspoon gluten-free jerk seasoning (dry)

1 tablespoon chopped fresh parsley

1 Heat oil in 10-inch nonstick skillet over medium heat. Cook onion and sweet potatoes in oil about 5 minutes, stirring occasionally, until light brown; reduce heat to low. Cover and cook 10 to 12 minutes, stirring occasionally, until potatoes are tender.

2 Stir in brown sugar and jerk seasoning. Cook uncovered about 3 minutes, stirring occasionally, until glazed. Sprinkle with parsley.

1 Serving: Calories 130 (Calories from Fat 10); Total Fat 1.5g (Saturated Fat 0g; Trans Fat 0g); Cholesterol 0mg; Sodium 35mg; Total Carbohydrate 27g (Dietary Fiber 3g); Protein 2g **% Daily Value:** Vitamin A 350%; Vitamin C 15%; Calcium 4%; Iron 4% **Exchanges:** ½ Starch, 1 Other Carbohydrate, ½ Vegetable, ½ Fat **Carbohydrate Choices:** 2

Vitamin A from sweet potatoes is a powerful antioxidant that helps with healthy vision, particularly at night.

Coconut-Ginger Rice

Prep Time: 10 Minutes • Start to Finish: 30 Minutes • 8 servings

2½ cups Progresso® reduced-sodium chicken broth (from 32-oz carton)

⅔ cup reduced-fat (lite) coconut milk (not cream of coconut)

1 tablespoon grated gingerroot

½ teaspoon salt

1⅓ cups uncooked regular long-grain white rice

1 teaspoon grated lime peel

3 medium green onions, chopped (3 tablespoons)

3 tablespoons flaked coconut, toasted

Lime slices

1 In 3-quart saucepan, heat broth, coconut milk, gingerroot and salt to boiling over medium-high heat. Stir in rice. Return to boiling. Reduce heat; cover and simmer about 15 minutes or until rice is tender and liquid is absorbed. Remove from heat.

2 Add lime peel and onions; fluff rice mixture lightly with fork to mix. Garnish with coconut and lime slices.

1 Serving: Calories 150 (Calories from Fat 20); Total Fat 2g (Saturated Fat 1.5g; Trans Fat 0g); Cholesterol 0mg; Sodium 340mg; Total Carbohydrate 30g (Dietary Fiber 0g); Protein 3g **% Daily Value:** Vitamin A 0%; Vitamin C 2%; Calcium 0%; Iron 8% **Exchanges:** 1 Starch, 1 Other Carbohydrate **Carbohydrate Choices:** 2

If you don't use fresh gingerroot quickly, tightly wrap and freeze it, unpeeled, up to 6 months. To use frozen gingerroot, slice off a piece and return the rest to the freezer.

To toast coconut, spread evenly on ungreased cookie sheet and bake in 350°F oven for 5 to 7 minutes, stirring occasionally, until golden brown.

Gravy

Prep Time: 5 Minutes • Start to Finish: 10 Minutes • 4 (¼ cup each)

1 tablespoon poultry or meat drippings, melted ghee or olive oil

1 tablespoon white rice flour

¼ teaspoon salt

1 cup gluten-free almond, rice, soy or regular milk

1 teaspoon gluten-free browning and seasoning sauce

1 In 1-quart saucepan, beat drippings, flour and salt with whisk until well mixed. Gradually beat in milk, cooking and stirring over medium heat about 5 minutes or until thickened. Remove from heat; beat in browning and seasoning sauce.

1 Serving: Calories 70 (Calories from Fat 40); Total Fat 4.5g (Saturated Fat 1g; Trans Fat 0g); Cholesterol 0mg; Sodium 170mg; Total Carbohydrate 6g (Dietary Fiber 0g); Protein 2g **% Daily Value:** Vitamin A 2%; Vitamin C 0%; Calcium 8%; Iron 0% **Exchanges:** ½ Skim Milk, ½ Fat **Carbohydrate Choices:** ½

Contributed by Jean Duane Alternative Cook http://www.alternativecook.com

Use unsweetened or "original" flavored milk substitutes rather than "vanilla."

Look for gluten-free browning and seasoning sauce at natural grocery stores.

chapter 5

desserts & more

Delicious Chocolate Cake with White Frosting

Prep Time: 30 Minutes • Start to Finish: 2 Hours 15 Minutes • 12 servings

CAKE

- 1 tablespoon sweet white sorghum flour
- ½ cup sweet white sorghum flour
- ¾ cup potato starch flour
- ½ cup white rice flour
- ½ cup tapioca flour
- ¼ cup garbanzo and fava flour
- ½ cup unsweetened baking cocoa
- 1 teaspoon xanthan gum
- 1 teaspoon guar gum
- 1 teaspoon gluten-free baking powder
- 1 teaspoon baking soda
- ½ teaspoon salt
- ¾ cup sunflower or canola oil
- 1 cup brewed coffee (room temperature)
- 3 eggs
- 1½ cups granulated sugar
- 2 teaspoons apple cider vinegar
- 2 teaspoons pure vanilla

FROSTING

- 1 cup melted ghee or sunflower or canola oil
- 2 teaspoons pure vanilla
- ⅛ teaspoon salt
- 4 cups gluten-free powdered sugar
- 2 tablespoons almond milk, soymilk or regular milk

1 Heat oven to 350°F. Spray 2 (8-inch) round cake pans with cooking spray (without flour); sprinkle with 1 tablespoon sorghum flour.

2 In medium bowl, mix ½ cup sorghum flour, the remaining flours, the cocoa, xanthan gum, guar gum, baking powder, baking soda and ½ teaspoon salt with whisk; set aside. In large bowl, beat oil, coffee, eggs, granulated sugar, vinegar and 2 teaspoons vanilla with electric mixer on low speed until frothy. Gradually add flour mixture, beating on medium speed until well blended. Divide batter evenly between pans.

3 Bake 40 to 42 minutes or until toothpick inserted in center comes out clean. Cool in pans on cooling racks 30 minutes. Remove cakes from pans to cooling racks; cool completely, about 30 minutes.

4 In medium bowl, beat ghee, vanilla and ⅛ teaspoon salt with electric mixer on medium speed. Gradually add powdered sugar and milk, beating until thickened. Beat 4 minutes longer or until frosting is fluffy. On serving plate, place 1 cake layer; spread with frosting. Top with second cake layer; spread frosting over top and side of cake.

1 Serving: Calories 700 (Calories from Fat 310); Total Fat 34g (Saturated Fat 4g; Trans Fat 0g); Cholesterol 55mg; Sodium 290mg; Total Carbohydrate 92g (Dietary Fiber 3g); Protein 4g **% Daily Value:** Vitamin A 0%; Vitamin C 0%; Calcium 4%; Iron 8% **Exchanges:** 2 Starch, 4 Other Carbohydrate, 6½ Fat **Carbohydrate Choices:** 6

Contributed by Jean Duane Alternative Cook http://www.alternativecook.com

Coffee brings out the taste of chocolate, and brewed coffee is the secret ingredient in this cake. If you prefer, you can substitute 1 cup of water or, better yet, sparkling water.

Garbanzo bean flour adds fiber to a gluten-free diet; one serving of the cake is a good source of fiber.

Chocolate-Orange Cake with Ganache Glaze

Prep Time: 40 Minutes • Start to Finish: 2 Hours 30 Minutes • 10 servings

CAKE

1 box Betty Crocker® Gluten Free devil's food cake mix

1 cup water

½ cup butter, softened

3 whole eggs

FILLING

½ cup sugar

2 tablespoons cornstarch

½ cup orange juice

¼ cup water

2 egg yolks, lightly beaten

2 tablespoons butter

1½ teaspoons grated orange peel

GLAZE

6 oz semisweet baking chocolate, finely chopped

½ cup whipping cream

4 teaspoons butter

1 Heat oven to 350°F (325°F for dark or nonstick pan). Generously spray bottom only of 8- or 9-inch round cake pan with cooking spray (without flour).

2 In large bowl, beat cake mix, 1 cup water, ½ cup butter and the eggs with electric mixer on low speed 30 seconds, then on medium speed 2 minutes, scraping bowl occasionally. Pour batter into pan.

3 Bake 43 to 48 minutes or until toothpick inserted in center comes out clean. Cool 10 minutes. Run knife around edge of pan to loosen cake; remove from pan to cooling rack. Cool completely, about 1 hour.

4 Meanwhile, in 1-quart heavy saucepan, mix sugar and cornstarch. Gradually stir in orange juice, ¼ cup water and the egg yolks. Cook over medium heat, stirring constantly, until thickened. Cook and stir 1 minute longer. Remove from heat; stir in 2 tablespoons butter and the orange peel. Transfer filling to small bowl. Cover; refrigerate 30 minutes.

5 In medium bowl, place chocolate. In 1-quart saucepan, heat whipping cream and 4 teaspoons butter over medium heat until butter melts and mixture boils. Pour cream mixture over chocolate; stir until smooth. Cool on cooling rack 10 minutes or until room temperature.

6 Split cake horizontally to make 2 layers. On cut side of bottom layer, spread filling; cover with top layer. Pour glaze over top of cake; spread glaze to edge of cake and allow to drizzle down side of cake. Store in refrigerator.

1 Serving: Calories 490 (Calories from Fat 230); Total Fat 25g (Saturated Fat 15g; Trans Fat 0.5g); Cholesterol 150mg; Sodium 360mg; Total Carbohydrate 60g (Dietary Fiber 2g); Protein 4g **% Daily Value:** Vitamin A 15%; Vitamin C 4%; Calcium 4%; Iron 15% **Exchanges:** 1 Starch, 3 Other Carbohydrate, 5 Fat **Carbohydrate Choices:** 4

For a white chocolate glaze, substitute 6 oz white chocolate baking bars or squares for the semisweet chocolate.

For a smooth filling, mix the sugar and cornstarch thoroughly before adding liquid. This keeps the cornstarch from developing lumps during cooking.

Red Velvet Cake

Prep Time: 15 Minutes • Start to Finish: 1 Hour 55 Minutes • 12 servings

1   box Betty Crocker® Gluten Free devil's food cake mix

1   cup buttermilk

1   tablespoon gluten-free red food color

¼   teaspoon baking soda

½   cup butter, softened

3   eggs

1¼ cups Betty Crocker® Whipped cream cheese frosting (from 12-oz container)

     Unsweetened baking cocoa, if desired

1 Heat oven to 350°F (325°F for dark or nonstick pan). Generously spray bottom only of 8- or 9-inch square pan with cooking spray (without flour).

2 In large bowl, beat cake mix, buttermilk, food color, baking soda, butter and eggs with electric mixer on low speed 30 seconds, then on medium speed 2 minutes, scraping bowl occasionally. Pour batter into pan.

3 Bake 40 to 45 minutes or until toothpick inserted in center comes out clean. Cool on cooling rack 10 minutes. Run knife around edge of pan to loosen cake; remove from pan to cooling rack. Cool completely.

4 Place cake on serving plate. Frost top and sides of cake with cream cheese frosting; sprinkle with cocoa. Cut into 4 rows by 3 rows.

1 Serving: Calories 320 (Calories from Fat 130); Total Fat 14g (Saturated Fat 7g; Trans Fat 1.5g); Cholesterol 75mg; Sodium 350mg; Total Carbohydrate 44g (Dietary Fiber 0g); Protein 3g **% Daily Value:** Vitamin A 6%; Vitamin C 0%; Calcium 4%; Iron 8% **Exchanges:** 1 Starch, 2 Other Carbohydrate, 2½ Fat **Carbohydrate Choices:** 3

For Red Velvet Cupcakes, place a paper baking cup in each of 12 regular-size muffin cups. Make batter as directed and divide evenly among muffin cups. Bake 18 to 23 minutes or until toothpick inserted in center comes out clean. Cool 5 minutes; remove from pan to cooling rack. Frost cooled cupcakes.

Chocolate Cake with Praline Topping

Prep Time: 20 Minutes • Start to Finish: 2 Hours • 12 servings

CAKE

- **1 box Betty Crocker® Gluten Free devil's food cake mix**
- **1 cup water**
- **½ cup butter, softened**
- **3 eggs**

TOPPING

- **¼ cup butter or margarine**
- **1 cup packed brown sugar**
- **⅓ cup whipping cream**
- **1 cup gluten-free powdered sugar**
- **1 teaspoon pure vanilla**
- **1 cup chopped pecans, toasted**

1 Heat oven to 350°F (325°F for dark or nonstick pan). Spray bottom only of 8- or 9-inch square pan with cooking spray (without flour).

2 In large bowl, beat cake mix, water, ½ cup butter and the eggs with electric mixer on low speed 30 seconds, then on medium speed 2 minutes, scraping bowl occasionally. Pour batter into pan.

3 Bake 8-inch pan 44 to 49 minutes, 9-inch pan 38 to 43 minutes, or until toothpick inserted in center comes out clean. Cool on cooling rack 10 minutes. Run knife around edge of pan to loosen cake; remove from pan to cooling rack. Cool completely.

4 In 2-quart heavy saucepan, heat ¼ cup butter, the brown sugar and whipping cream to boiling, stirring frequently. Boil and stir 1 minute; remove from heat. Stir in powdered sugar and vanilla until smooth. Stir in pecans. Cool 10 to 15 minutes, stirring occasionally, until topping begins to thicken.

5 Spread warm topping over cake. Cool before serving. Cut into 4 rows by 3 rows.

1 Serving: Calories 450 (Calories from Fat 200); Total Fat 22g (Saturated Fat 10g; Trans Fat 0.5g); Cholesterol 90mg; Sodium 310mg; Total Carbohydrate 60g (Dietary Fiber 1g); Protein 3g **% Daily Value:** Vitamin A 10%; Vitamin C 0%; Calcium 4%; Iron 10% **Exchanges:** 1 Starch, 3 Other Carbohydrate, 4 Fat **Carbohydrate Choices:** 4

Gluten-free mixes make baking easy and successful for people with celiac disease.

To toast pecans, spread in ungreased shallow pan. Bake uncovered at 350°F 6 to 10 minutes, stirring occasionally, until light brown.

Chocolate Snack Cake with Creamy Butterscotch Frosting

Prep Time: 15 Minutes • Start to Finish: 2 Hours • 16 servings

CAKE

- ¼ **cup white rice flour**
- ¼ **cup tapioca flour**
- ¼ **cup potato starch flour**
- 3 **tablespoons sweet white sorghum flour**
- ¼ **cup unsweetened baking cocoa**
- 1 **teaspoon xanthan gum**
- 2 **teaspoons gluten-free baking powder**
- ½ **teaspoon salt**
- ½ **cup sunflower oil**
- ⅔ **cup almond butter**
- ½ **cup packed brown sugar**
- ½ **cup granulated sugar**
- 2 **eggs**
- ½ **cup water**

FROSTING

- ½ **cup packed dark brown sugar**
- ¼ **cup melted ghee**
- 3 **to 4 tablespoons almond milk**
- ⅛ **teaspoon salt**
- 1 **cup gluten-free powdered sugar**
- 2 **tablespoons sliced almonds**
- 2 **tablespoons miniature semisweet chocolate chips**

1 Heat oven to 350°F. Spray bottom and sides of 8-inch square pan with cooking spray (without flour).

2 In small bowl, mix flours, cocoa, xanthan gum, baking powder and ½ teaspoon salt with whisk; set aside. In medium bowl, beat oil, almond butter, ½ cup brown sugar, the granulated sugar, eggs and water with electric mixer on medium speed until well blended. Gradually add flour mixture, beating until well blended. Pour batter into pan.

3 Bake 30 to 35 minutes or until cake springs back when touched lightly in center. Cool completely in pan on cooling rack, about 1 hour.

4 Meanwhile, in 2-quart saucepan, place ½ cup brown sugar, ghee, 3 tablespoons of the milk and ⅛ teaspoon salt. Heat to boiling over medium heat about 3 to 4 minutes, stirring constantly. Remove from heat; beat in powdered sugar until frosting is smooth and spreadable. If frosting is too thick, stir in additional almond milk, 1 teaspoon at a time. Frost cake. Sprinkle almonds and chocolate chips over top. Cut into 4 rows by 4 rows.

1 Serving: Calories 330 (Calories from Fat 160); Total Fat 18g (Saturated Fat 3.5g; Trans Fat 0g); Cholesterol 35mg; Sodium 210mg; Total Carbohydrate 38g (Dietary Fiber 1g); Protein 3g **% Daily Value:** Vitamin A 2%; Vitamin C 0%; Calcium 8%; Iron 6% **Exchanges:** ½ Starch, 2 Other Carbohydrate, 3½ Fat **Carbohydrate Choices:** 2½

Contributed by Jean Duane Alternative Cook http://www.alternativecook.com

> **Gluten-free ingredients,** such as almond butter made from ground almonds, provide vitamin E and monounsaturated fat. Look for almond butter in the baking aisle of your grocery store.

Lemon-Filled Coconut Cake

Prep Time: 25 Minutes • Start to Finish: 2 Hours 25 Minutes • 10 servings

CAKE

- 1 box Betty Crocker® Gluten Free yellow cake mix
- ½ cup butter, softened
- ⅔ cup water
- 2 teaspoons pure vanilla
- 3 eggs

FROSTING

- 2 cups gluten-free powdered sugar
- ¼ cup butter, softened
- 1 teaspoon gluten-free coconut extract, if desired
- 1 to 2 tablespoons milk

FILLING

- ½ cup lemon curd
- 1 cup flaked coconut, toasted

1 Heat oven to 350°F (325°F for dark or nonstick pan). Spray bottom only of 8- or 9-inch round pan with cooking spray (without flour).

2 In large bowl, beat all cake ingredients with electric mixer on low speed 30 seconds, then on medium speed 2 minutes, scraping bowl occasionally. Pour batter into pan.

3 Bake 41 to 46 minutes or until toothpick inserted in center comes out clean. Cool on cooling rack 10 minutes. Run knife around side of pan to loosen cake; remove from pan to cooling rack. Cool completely, about 1 hour.

4 In medium bowl, beat powdered sugar and ¼ cup butter with electric mixer on low speed. Stir in coconut extract and 1 tablespoon milk. Gradually beat in just enough remaining milk, 1 teaspoon at a time, until frosting is smooth and spreadable.

5 Split cake horizontally to make 2 layers. On cut side of bottom layer, spread lemon curd; top with ½ cup of the coconut. Cover with top layer. Frost top and side of cake with frosting. Sprinkle coconut over top of cake. Refrigerate loosely covered.

1 Serving: Calories 500 (Calories from Fat 190); Total Fat 21g (Saturated Fat 14g; Trans Fat 0.5g); Cholesterol 110mg; Sodium 360mg; Total Carbohydrate 72g (Dietary Fiber 1g); Protein 3g **% Daily Value:** Vitamin A 10%; Vitamin C 0%; Calcium 0%; Iron 2% **Exchanges:** 1½ Starch, 3½ Other Carbohydrate, 4 Fat **Carbohydrate Choices:** 5

> **To toast coconut,** spread in ungreased shallow pan. Bake uncovered at 350°F for 5 to 7 minutes, stirring occasionally, until golden brown.

Berries 'n' Cream Cake

Prep Time: 20 Minutes • Start to Finish: 1 Hour 15 Minutes • 9 servings

CAKE

- 1 box Betty Crocker® Gluten Free yellow cake mix
- ⅛ teaspoon ground nutmeg
- ½ cup cold butter or margarine
- ⅔ cup milk
- 2 teaspoons pure vanilla
- 2 eggs

BERRIES

- 6 cups mixed fresh berries (blueberries, raspberries, sliced strawberries)
- ½ cup granulated sugar

SWEETENED WHIPPED CREAM

- 1½ cups whipping cream
- 3 tablespoons gluten-free powdered sugar

1 Heat oven to 375°F (350°F for dark or nonstick pan). Spray bottom only of 8- or 9-inch square pan with cooking spray (without flour).

2 In large bowl, stir cake mix and nutmeg. Cut in butter, using pastry blender (or pulling 2 table knives through ingredients in opposite directions), until crumbly. In small bowl, whisk milk, vanilla and eggs; stir into crumb mixture until moistened. Spread in pan.

3 Bake 30 to 35 minutes or until toothpick inserted in center comes out clean.

4 Meanwhile, in another large bowl, stir together berries and granulated sugar; set aside to allow juices to form.

5 Cool cake on cooling rack 10 minutes. Run knife around edge of pan to loosen cake. Cool at least 10 minutes longer. In chilled large bowl, beat whipping cream and powdered sugar with electric mixer on low speed until mixture begins to thicken. Gradually increase speed to high, beating just until soft peaks form.

6 Cut cake into 3 rows by 3 rows. Cut each piece horizontally in half. Spoon half of the berries and sweetened whipped cream over bottom cake pieces; cover with top cake pieces. Spoon remaining berries and whipped cream over cake.

1 Serving: Calories 510 (Calories from Fat 220); Total Fat 24g (Saturated Fat 15g; Trans Fat 1g); Cholesterol 120mg; Sodium 360mg; Total Carbohydrate 68g (Dietary Fiber 3g); Protein 5g **% Daily Value:** Vitamin A 15%; Vitamin C 25%; Calcium 8%; Iron 4% **Exchanges:** 2 Starch, ½ Fruit, 2 Other Carbohydrate, 4½ Fat **Carbohydrate Choices:** 4½

A colorful mixture of berries tops this dessert offering a good source of fiber—without gluten. If you like, substitute a scoop of gluten-free vanilla ice cream for the sweetened whipped cream.

Cranberry Upside-Down Cake

Prep Time: 20 Minutes • Start to Finish: 1 Hour 50 Minutes • 8 servings

CAKE

- 1½ cups sweetened dried cranberries
- 1 cup water
- 2 tablespoons granulated sugar
- 1 tablespoon cornstarch
- ½ teaspoon ground cinnamon
- ⅛ teaspoon ground cloves
- ⅛ teaspoon ground nutmeg
- 1 teaspoon pure vanilla
- ½ cup cornmeal
- ¼ cup almond flour
- ¼ cup sweet white sorghum flour
- ¼ teaspoon xanthan gum
- ¼ teaspoon gluten-free baking powder
- ⅛ teaspoon salt
- ½ cup melted ghee or sunflower or canola oil
- 3 eggs
- ¼ cup packed brown sugar

SWEETENED WHIPPED CREAM

- ½ cup whipping cream
- 1 tablespoon granulated sugar
- ½ teaspoon pure vanilla

1 Heat oven to 350°F. Spray 8-inch round cake pan with cooking spray (without flour).

2 In 2-quart saucepan, stir cranberries, water, 2 tablespoons granulated sugar, the cornstarch, cinnamon, cloves and nutmeg. Cook on high heat, stirring constantly with whisk until mixture boils; boil and stir 1 minute longer until thickened. Remove from heat; stir in 1 teaspoon vanilla. Spoon into pan.

3 In small bowl, mix cornmeal, flours, xanthan gum, baking powder and salt with whisk; set aside. In medium bowl, beat ghee, eggs and brown sugar with electric mixer on medium speed until blended. Gradually add flour mixture, beating until well blended. Spoon mixture on cranberry filling in pan; gently spread to cover.

4 Bake 20 minutes. Cover cake with cooking parchment paper; bake 5 to 10 minutes longer or until edges are golden brown and center is set. Cool on cooling rack 1 hour. Invert cake onto serving plate.

5 In chilled medium bowl, beat whipping cream, 1 tablespoon granulated sugar and ½ teaspoon vanilla with electric mixer on low speed until mixture begins to thicken. Gradually increase speed to high, beating just until soft peaks form. Cut cake into slices; top each slice with 2 tablespoons whipped cream.

1 Serving: Calories 340 (Calories from Fat 150); Total Fat 17g (Saturated Fat 9g; Trans Fat 0.5g); Cholesterol 110mg; Sodium 80mg; Total Carbohydrate 42g (Dietary Fiber 2g); Protein 4g **% Daily Value:** Vitamin A 10%; Vitamin C 0%; Calcium 4%; Iron 6% **Exchanges:** 1 Starch, 2 Other Carbohydrate, 3½ Fat **Carbohydrate Choices:** 3

For Blueberry Upside-Down Cake, substitute dried sweetened blueberries for the cranberries and add ½ teaspoon grated lemon peel.

Gluten-Free All-Purpose Flour Blend

Prep Time: 5 Minutes · Start to Finish: 5 Minutes · 4 pounds (13 cups)

3¾ cups brown rice flour

3¾ cups white rice flour

3¾ cups tapioca flour

1¾ cups plus 2 tablespoons potato starch flour

2 tablespoons plus 1½ teaspoons xanthan gum

3¾ teaspoons salt

1 In large bowl, mix all ingredients with whisk until fully incorporated. Transfer to storage container; seal tightly. Store in cool, dry place or in refrigerator. Before using, stir to blend the flours and xanthan gum.

Contributed by Silvana Nardone Silvana's Kitchen http://silvanaskitchen.com

Use this flour blend in Boston Cream Pie (page 197), Cinnamon Roll Pound Cake with Vanilla Drizzle (page 198) and Hazelnut Streusel Coffee Cake (page 55).

Want a featherlight blend? Swap out some of the brown rice flour for more white rice flour.

Boston Cream Pie

Prep Time: 30 Minutes • Start to Finish: 3 Hours 15 Minutes • 16 servings

CAKE

1¾ cups almond flour

1¼ cups Gluten-Free All-Purpose Flour Blend (page 195)

2 teaspoons gluten-free baking powder

½ teaspoon salt

1½ cups sugar

1 cup water

½ cup butter, melted

3 whole eggs

2 teaspoons pure vanilla

CUSTARD

1¼ cups whole milk

¼ cup sugar

2 egg yolks

2 tablespoons cornstarch

¼ teaspoon salt

1 tablespoon butter, cut into small pieces

1 teaspoon pure vanilla

GLAZE

4 oz dark baking chocolate, chopped

3 tablespoons butter, cut into small pieces

1 tablespoon light corn syrup

1 Heat oven to 350°F. Spray 2 (8-inch) round cake pans with cooking spray (without flour).

2 In medium bowl, mix almond flour, flour blend, baking powder and ½ teaspoon salt; set aside. In large bowl, beat 1½ cups sugar, the water, melted butter, the eggs and 2 teaspoons vanilla with electric mixer on low speed 1 minute. Gradually add flour mixture, beating on medium speed 2 minutes. Divide batter evenly between pans.

3 Bake 27 to 30 minutes or until golden and toothpick inserted in center comes out clean. Cool on cooling rack 15 minutes; remove from pans to cooling racks. Cool completely.

4 Meanwhile, in 2-quart heavy saucepan, stir milk, ¼ cup sugar, the egg yolks, cornstarch and ¼ teaspoon salt. Heat to boiling over medium heat, stirring constantly; boil 1 minute until thickened and mixture coats back of spoon. Remove from heat; stir in 1 tablespoon butter and 1 teaspoon vanilla until smooth. Cover surface of custard with plastic wrap. Refrigerate until set, about 2 hours.

5 In small microwavable bowl, microwave glaze ingredients uncovered on High 1 minute; stir until chocolate is melted and mixture is smooth.

6 To assemble, invert one cake layer onto serving platter. Stir cold custard; spread on top of cake just to edge. Top with second cake layer. Slowly pour glaze over cake, spreading to cover and letting it drip down side. Slice cake gently with serrated knife.

1 Serving: Calories 380 (Calories from Fat 190); Total Fat 21g (Saturated Fat 9g; Trans Fat 0g); Cholesterol 90mg; Sodium 270mg; Total Carbohydrate 41g (Dietary Fiber 3g); Protein 6g **% Daily Value:** Vitamin A 8%; Vitamin C 0%; Calcium 10%; Iron 10% **Exchanges:** 1½ Starch, 1½ Other Carbohydrate, 4 Fat **Carbohydrate Choices:** 3

Contributed by Silvana Nardone Silvana's Kitchen http://silvanaskitchen.com

Almond flour (made from finely ground almonds) contains zinc, a mineral that helps us taste and smell.

Cinnamon Roll Pound Cake with Vanilla Drizzle

Prep Time: 25 Minutes • Start to Finish: 2 Hours 30 Minutes • 8 servings

2 cups Gluten-Free All-Purpose Flour Blend (page 195)

2 teaspoons gluten-free baking powder

½ teaspoon salt

1 cup butter, softened

¾ cup granulated sugar

4 eggs

2½ teaspoons pure vanilla

1 tablespoon ground cinnamon

½ cup gluten-free powdered sugar

1 tablespoon milk

1 Heat oven to 350°F. Spray 9x5-inch loaf pan with cooking spray (without flour).

2 In small bowl, mix flour blend, baking powder and salt; set aside. In large bowl, beat butter and granulated sugar with electric mixer on medium-high speed until fluffy, about 3 minutes. Reduce speed to medium-low; gradually beat in eggs and 2 teaspoons of the vanilla until blended. Gradually add flour mixture, beating on low speed just until combined.

3 Transfer half the batter to small bowl; stir in cinnamon. Alternately spoon plain batter and cinnamon batter into pan and swirl with knife.

4 Bake 40 to 50 minutes or until toothpick inserted in center comes out clean. Cool on cooling rack 15 minutes; remove from pan to cooling rack. Cool completely, about 1 hour.

5 In small bowl, mix powdered sugar, milk and remaining ½ teaspoon vanilla until smooth. Drizzle over cake.

1 Serving: Calories 480 (Calories from Fat 240); Total Fat 26g (Saturated Fat 16g; Trans Fat 1g); Cholesterol 165mg; Sodium 480mg; Total Carbohydrate 54g (Dietary Fiber 2g); Protein 5g **% Daily Value:** Vitamin A 15%; Vitamin C 0%; Calcium 10%; Iron 4% **Exchanges:** 1½ Starch, 2 Other Carbohydrate, 5 Fat **Carbohydrate Choices:** 3½

Contributed by Silvana Nardone Silvana's Kitchen http://silvanaskitchen.com

Have the eggs at room temperature when making this cake. If you forget to take them out of the refrigerator, just place them in a bowl and cover with warm water to take the chill off.

Spicy Pumpkin Cake

Prep Time: 30 Minutes • Start to Finish: 3 Hours 45 Minutes • 16 servings

¾ cup tapioca flour

¾ cup potato starch flour

½ cup white rice flour

½ cup finely ground almond flour

¼ cup sweet white sorghum flour

¼ cup garbanzo and fava flour

1 teaspoon xanthan gum

1 teaspoon guar gum

2 teaspoons gluten-free baking powder

½ teaspoon salt

1 teaspoon ground cinnamon

1 teaspoon ground ginger

⅛ teaspoon ground nutmeg

⅛ teaspoon ground cloves

3 eggs

1 cup sunflower or canola oil

¼ cup almond milk, soymilk or regular milk

¾ cup canned pumpkin (not pumpkin pie mix)

1½ cups granulated sugar

2 teaspoons pure vanilla

1 teaspoon apple cider vinegar

2 tablespoons gluten-free powdered sugar

1 Heat oven to 350°F. Spray 10-inch nonstick fluted tube cake pan with cooking spray (without flour).

2 In medium bowl, mix flours, xanthan gum, guar gum, baking powder, salt, cinnamon, ginger, nutmeg and cloves with whisk; set aside. In large bowl, beat eggs, oil, milk, pumpkin, granulated sugar, vanilla and vinegar with electric mixer on low speed until smooth. Gradually add flour mixture, beating on medium speed 2 minutes until well blended. Pour batter into pan.

3 Bake 30 minutes. Cover cake with cooking parchment paper; bake 25 to 30 minutes longer or until toothpick inserted in center comes out clean. Cool 15 minutes; remove from pan to cooling rack. Cool completely, about 2 hours. Sprinkle cake with powdered sugar.

1 Serving: Calories 330 (Calories from Fat 150); Total Fat 17g (Saturated Fat 2g; Trans Fat 0g); Cholesterol 40mg; Sodium 150mg; Total Carbohydrate 40g (Dietary Fiber 2g); Protein 3g **% Daily Value:** Vitamin A 35%; Vitamin C 0%; Calcium 6%; Iron 4% **Exchanges:** 1 Starch, 1½ Other Carbohydrate, 3½ Fat **Carbohydrate Choices:** 2½

Contributed by Jean Duane Alternative Cook http://www.alternativecook.com

Serve this cake during the holidays for a delicious alternative to pumpkin pie.

Better-Than-Almost-Anything Cake

Prep Time: 20 Minutes • Start to Finish: 3 Hours • 9 servings

1 box Betty Crocker® Gluten Free devil's food cake mix

Water, butter and eggs called for on cake mix box

1 jar (12.25 oz) gluten-free caramel topping

1 cup frozen (thawed) whipped topping

½ cup gluten-free toffee bits

1 Heat oven to 350°F (or 325°F for dark or nonstick pan). Make and bake cake mix as directed on box, using water, butter, eggs and any of the pan choices.

2 With handle of wooden spoon, poke top of warm cake every ½ inch. Drizzle caramel topping evenly over top of cake; let stand until absorbed into cake. Cover; refrigerate about 2 hours or until chilled.

3 Spread whipped topping over top of cake. Sprinkle with toffee bits. Store covered in refrigerator.

1 Serving: Calories 520 (Calories from Fat 180); Total Fat 21g (Saturated Fat 13g; Trans Fat 0.5g); Cholesterol 115mg; Sodium 520mg; Total Carbohydrate 80g (Dietary Fiber 1g); Protein 4g **% Daily Value:** Vitamin A 15%; Vitamin C 0%; Calcium 4%; Iron 10% **Exchanges:** 1½ Starch, 4 Other Carbohydrate, 4 Fat **Carbohydrate Choices:** 5

> **The caramel topping** will be easier to drizzle if it has been kept at room temperature. If it's been refrigerated, remove the lid and microwave on High about 15 seconds.

Vanilla Cupcakes with Caramel–Sea Salt Frosting

Prep Time: 25 Minutes • Start to Finish: 1 Hour 55 Minutes • 12 cupcakes

CUPCAKES

- 1 box Betty Crocker® Gluten Free yellow cake mix
- ½ cup butter, softened
- ⅔ cup water
- 2 teaspoons pure vanilla
- 3 eggs

FROSTING

- ¼ cup butter
- ⅔ cup packed brown sugar
- 2 tablespoons milk
- ½ teaspoon pure vanilla
- 1 cup gluten-free powdered sugar
- ¼ teaspoon coarse sea salt

1 Heat oven to 350°F (325°F for dark or nonstick pan). Place paper baking cup in each of 12 regular-size muffin cups.

2 In large bowl, beat all cupcake ingredients with electric mixer on low speed 30 seconds, then on medium speed 2 minutes, scraping bowl occasionally. Divide batter evenly among muffin cups.

3 Bake 18 to 23 minutes or until toothpick inserted in center comes out clean. Cool 5 minutes; remove from pan to cooling rack. Cool completely, about 1 hour.

4 Meanwhile, in 2-quart heavy saucepan, melt ¼ cup butter over medium heat. Stir in brown sugar with whisk. Heat to boiling, stirring constantly. Stir in milk. Return to boiling. Remove from heat; cool until lukewarm, about 30 minutes. Stir in ½ teaspoon vanilla; gradually stir in powdered sugar until spreadable (add additional milk if frosting becomes too thick). Frost cupcakes. Sprinkle with sea salt.

1 Serving: Calories 340 (Calories from Fat 120); Total Fat 13g (Saturated Fat 8g; Trans Fat 0g); Cholesterol 85mg; Sodium 340mg; Total Carbohydrate 53g (Dietary Fiber 0g); Protein 2g **% Daily Value:** Vitamin A 8%; Vitamin C 0%; Calcium 2%; Iron 0% **Exchanges:** 1 Starch, 2½ Other Carbohydrate, 2½ Fat **Carbohydrate Choices:** 3½

When purchasing sea salt for this recipe, look for a coarse-textured, minimally refined sea salt, such as Himalayan pink salt or black salt. Sprinkle salt on cupcakes immediately after frosting each one so salt adheres to frosting before it stiffens.

Brownie Cupcakes with Chocolate Fudge Frosting

Prep Time: 30 Minutes • Start to Finish: 1 Hour 30 Minutes • 12 cupcakes

CUPCAKES

¼ cup brown rice flour

¼ cup sweet white sorghum flour

2 tablespoons tapioca flour

¾ cup granulated sugar

¾ teaspoon gluten-free baking powder

¼ teaspoon salt

1½ cups miniature semisweet chocolate chips

¼ cup unsweetened baking cocoa

⅓ cup canola oil

3 tablespoons water

3 eggs

FROSTING

1⅓ cups miniature semisweet chocolate chips

¼ cup butter, cut into small pieces

½ cup whipping cream

2 cups gluten-free powdered sugar

1 Heat oven to 350°F. Place paper baking cup in each of 12 regular-size muffin cups; spray cups with cooking spray (without flour).

2 In small bowl, mix flours, granulated sugar, baking powder, salt and ½ cup of the chocolate chips with whisk; set aside. In medium microwavable bowl, microwave cocoa, oil, water and remaining 1 cup chocolate chips on High 1 minute or until chips are almost melted. Stir with whisk until smooth. Cool to room temperature, about 3 minutes. Stir in eggs and flour mixture until batter is smooth and shiny. Divide batter evenly among muffin cups.

3 Bake 25 minutes or until set. Cool on cooling rack 15 minutes; remove from pan to cooling rack. Cool completely.

4 Meanwhile, in large microwavable bowl, microwave 1⅓ cups chocolate chips, the butter and whipping cream on High 1 minute. Stir until smooth. Cool 8 minutes. Add powdered sugar; beat with electric mixer on high speed 3 to 5 minutes or until smooth and creamy. Refrigerate 10 minutes. Pipe or spread frosting over cupcakes.

1 Serving: Calories 520 (Calories from Fat 250); Total Fat 27g (Saturated Fat 13g; Trans Fat 0g); Cholesterol 75mg; Sodium 105mg; Total Carbohydrate 65g (Dietary Fiber 3g); Protein 4g **% Daily Value:** Vitamin A 6%; Vitamin C 0%; Calcium 4%; Iron 10% **Exchanges:** 1 Starch, 3½ Other Carbohydrate, 5 Fat **Carbohydrate Choices:** 4

Contributed by Silvana Nardone Silvana's Kitchen http://silvanaskitchen.com

Want more cupcakes for later? Make a double batch of the batter and freeze half of the baked, unfrosted cupcakes in a resealable freezer plastic bag up to 1 month. When ready to eat, thaw at room temperature about 20 minutes while making the frosting.

Banana Cupcakes with Browned Butter Frosting

Prep Time: 20 Minutes • Start to Finish: 1 Hour 10 Minutes • 17 cupcakes

CUPCAKES

- 1 **box Betty Crocker® Gluten Free yellow cake mix**
- 1 **cup mashed ripe bananas (2 medium)**
- ⅓ **cup butter, melted***
- ⅓ **cup water**
- 3 **eggs, beaten**
- 2 **teaspoons pure vanilla**

FROSTING

- ⅓ **cup butter***
- 3 **cups gluten-free powdered sugar**
- 1 **teaspoon pure vanilla**
- 3 **to 4 tablespoons milk**

1 Heat oven to 350°F. Place paper baking cup in each of 17 regular-size muffin cups. In a bowl, stir cupcake ingredients until ingredients are moist. Spoon batter evenly into muffin cups.

2 Bake 16 to 18 minutes or until golden brown. Remove from pan to cooling rack. Cool completely, about 30 minutes.

3 In small saucepan, heat ⅓ cup butter over medium heat just until light brown, stirring occasionally. Remove from heat. Cool slightly, about 5 minutes.

4 In medium bowl, beat butter, powdered sugar, vanilla and enough milk until smooth and spreadable. Spread frosting over cooled cupcakes.

*Do not use margarine or vegetable oil spreads.

1 Cupcake: Calories 270 (Calories from Fat 70); Total Fat 8g (Saturated Fat 5g; Trans Fat 0g); Cholesterol 55mg; Sodium 200mg; Total Carbohydrate 46g (Dietary Fiber 0g); Protein 2g **% Daily Value:** Vitamin A 6%; Vitamin C 0%; Calcium 0%; Iron 0% **Exchanges:** ½ Starch, 2½ Other Carbohydrate, 1½ Fat **Carbohydrate Choices:** 3

Beurre noisette is the French term for "browned butter," referring to butter that becomes light hazelnut in color during cooking. The wonderful, unforgettable, one-of-kind flavor has no equal or substitution.

Lemon Lover's Cupcakes with Lemon Buttercream Frosting

Prep Time: 20 Minutes • Start to Finish: 1 Hour 25 Minutes • 12 cupcakes

CUPCAKES

1 **box Betty Crocker® Gluten Free yellow cake mix**

⅔ **cup water**

½ **cup butter, melted**

2 **tablespoons grated lemon peel**

3 **eggs, beaten**

FROSTING

2 **cups gluten-free powdered sugar**

¼ **cup butter, softened**

2 **to 3 tablespoons fresh lemon juice**

1 **teaspoon grated lemon peel**

1 Heat oven to 350°F. Place paper baking cup in each of 12 regular-size muffin cups. In large bowl, stir cake mix, water, melted butter, the lemon peel and eggs just until dry ingredients are moistened. Divide batter evenly among muffin cups.

2 Bake 18 to 23 minutes or until toothpick inserted in center comes out clean. Cool 10 minutes. Remove from pan to cooling rack; cool completely, about 30 minutes.

3 In medium bowl, beat powdered sugar, ¼ cup butter and 1 tablespoon of the lemon juice with electric mixer on low speed until mixed. Add remaining lemon juice, 1 teaspoon at a time, until creamy and smooth. Beat in 1 teaspoon lemon peel. Frost cupcakes with frosting.

1 Cupcake: Calories 330 (Calories from Fat 120); Total Fat 13g (Saturated Fat 8g; Trans Fat 0g); Cholesterol 85mg; Sodium 290mg; Total Carbohydrate 51g (Dietary Fiber 0g); Protein 2g **% Daily Value:** Vitamin A 8%; Vitamin C 0%; Calcium 0%; Iron 0% **Exchanges:** ½ Starch, 3 Other Carbohydrate, 2½ Fat **Carbohydrate Choices:** 3½

Grate only the bright yellow portion of the lemon peel for the best flavor. The pith, or white part of the skin, is bitter.

Lemon Poppy Seed Cupcakes with Lemon Buttery Frosting

Prep Time: 30 Minutes • Start to Finish: 2 Hours • 24 cupcakes

CUPCAKES

- ¾ cup white rice flour
- ¾ cup tapioca flour
- ¾ cup potato starch flour
- ½ cup sweet white sorghum flour
- ¼ cup garbanzo and fava flour
- 1 teaspoon xanthan gum
- 2 teaspoons baking soda
- 1 teaspoon gluten-free baking powder
- ½ teaspoon salt
- 2 tablespoons poppy seed
- 2 eggs
- ½ cup gluten-free mayonnaise
- 2 teaspoons pure vanilla
- ¾ cup almond milk, soymilk or regular milk
- 2 teaspoons grated lemon peel
- ½ cup fresh lemon juice
- ¼ cup water
- 1¼ cups granulated sugar

FROSTING

- 1 cup melted ghee
- 2 teaspoons pure vanilla
- ⅛ teaspoon salt
- 4 cups gluten-free powdered sugar
- 1 to 2 tablespoons almond milk
- 2 teaspoons grated lemon peel
- 2 tablespoons fresh lemon juice

1 Heat oven to 350°F. Place paper baking cup in each of 24 regular-size muffin cups.

2 In medium bowl, mix flours, xanthan gum, baking soda, baking powder, ½ teaspoon salt and the poppy seed with whisk; set aside. In large bowl, beat eggs, mayonnaise, 2 teaspoons vanilla, ¾ cup milk, 2 teaspoons lemon peel, ½ cup lemon juice, the water and granulated sugar with electric mixer on low speed until frothy. Gradually add flour mixture, beating on low speed 2 minutes or until well blended. Divide batter evenly among muffin cups, filling each about three-fourths full.

3 Bake 25 to 27 minutes or until tops spring back when touched lightly in center. Remove from pans to cooling racks; cool completely, about 1 hour.

4 In medium bowl, beat ghee, 2 teaspoons vanilla and ⅛ teaspoon salt with electric mixer on medium speed. Gradually add powdered sugar and 1 tablespoon milk, beating until thickened. Add 2 teaspoons lemon peel and 2 tablespoons lemon juice; beat 4 minutes or until fluffy. Beat in remaining 1 tablespoon milk, 1 teaspoon at a time, until frosting is desired consistency. Frost cupcakes.

1 Cupcake: Calories 310 (Calories from Fat 120); Total Fat 13g (Saturated Fat 6g; Trans Fat 0g); Cholesterol 40mg; Sodium 230mg; Total Carbohydrate 46g (Dietary Fiber 1g); Protein 2g **% Daily Value:** Vitamin A 6%; Vitamin C 4%; Calcium 4%; Iron 2% **Exchanges:** 1 Starch, 2 Other Carbohydrate, 2½ Fat **Carbohydrate Choices:** 3

Contributed by Jean Duane Alternative Cook http://www.alternativecook.com

Sprinkle the frosted cupcakes with colorful sprinkles or freshly grated lemon peel or add a little gluten-free yellow food color to the frosting and stack these cupcakes on a cupcake tree for a centerpiece at a special luncheon or party.

Triple-Berry Mini Cheesecakes

Prep Time: 20 Minutes • Start to Finish: 4 Hours 45 Minutes • 12 mini cheesecakes

CRUST

1½ cups Cinnamon Chex® or Chocolate Chex® cereal, crushed to 1 cup

2 tablespoons sugar

2 tablespoons butter or margarine, melted

FILLING

1 package (8 oz) ⅓-less-fat cream cheese (Neufchâtel), softened

⅓ cup sugar

1 egg

2 containers (6 oz each) Yoplait® Original 99% Fat Free strawberry yogurt

2 teaspoons cornstarch

TOPPING

2 cups fresh berries (such as sliced strawberries, raspberries and/or blueberries)

¼ cup semisweet chocolate chips

1 Heat oven to 300°F. Place paper baking cup in each of 12 regular-size muffin cups. In medium bowl, mix crust ingredients. Press about 1 tablespoon crust mixture into bottom of each muffin cup.

2 In another medium bowl, beat cream cheese with electric mixer on medium speed until smooth. Add ⅓ cup sugar and the egg. Beat on medium speed about 2 minutes or until smooth. Add yogurt and cornstarch. Beat on low speed until smooth. Spoon about 3 tablespoons mixture into each muffin cup.

3 Bake 20 to 25 minutes or until edges are firm and center is jiggly. Turn off oven; cool in oven 30 minutes with door closed. Remove from oven; place on cooling rack. Cool at room temperature 30 minutes. Cover; refrigerate at least 3 hours.

4 Remove cheesecakes from muffin cups. Top each with fresh fruit. In small microwavable bowl, microwave chocolate chips uncovered on High 30 to 60 seconds, stirring every 15 seconds, until melted and smooth. Drizzle over fruit.

1 Mini Cheesecake: Calories 180 (Calories from Fat 80); Total Fat 9g (Saturated Fat 5g; Trans Fat 0g); Cholesterol 40mg; Sodium 140mg; Total Carbohydrate 23g (Dietary Fiber 0g); Protein 4g **% Daily Value:** Vitamin A 10%; Vitamin C 15%; Calcium 8%; Iron 10% **Exchanges:** 1 Starch, ½ Other Carbohydrate, 1½ Fat **Carbohydrate Choices:** 1½

Make these cheesecakes (without the topping) up to 1 month ahead of time and freeze in a labeled airtight container. About 3 hours before serving, place covered cheesecakes in the refrigerator to thaw. Add the topping just before serving.

Chocolate Chip Cookie Cheesecake

Prep Time: 20 Minutes • Start to Finish: 3 Hours 50 Minutes • 16 servings

CRUST

1 box Betty Crocker® Gluten Free chocolate chip cookie mix

Butter, pure vanilla and egg as called for on cookie mix box

FILLING

3 packages (8 oz each) cream cheese, softened

1¼ cups sugar

2 teaspoons pure vanilla

4 eggs

½ cup miniature semisweet chocolate chips

Unsweetened baking cocoa, if desired

1 Heat oven to 325°F. For crust, make cookie dough as directed on box, using butter, vanilla and egg. Press dough into bottom and 1 inch up side of ungreased 10-inch springform pan. Set aside.

2 For filling, in large bowl, beat cream cheese and sugar with electric mixer on low speed 30 seconds or until blended. Beat in vanilla and eggs, one at a time. Stir in chocolate chips. Pour into pan.

3 Bake 1 hour to 1 hour 15 minutes or until puffed and light golden brown. Turn oven off; let cake stand in oven 15 minutes with door open at least 4 inches. Remove from oven; run knife around inside edge of pan. Cool completely on cooling rack, at least 2 hours. Sprinkle with cocoa. Store any remaining cheesecake covered in refrigerator.

1 Serving: Calories 460 (Calories from Fat 230); Total Fat 26g (Saturated Fat 15g; Trans Fat 0.5g); Cholesterol 130mg; Sodium 350mg; Total Carbohydrate 50g (Dietary Fiber 0g); Protein 6g **% Daily Value:** Vitamin A 15%; Vitamin C 0%; Calcium 8%; Iron 2% **Exchanges:** 1 Starch, 2½ Other Carbohydrate, ½ High-Fat Meat, 4 Fat **Carbohydrate Choices:** 3

Cooling the baked cheesecake slowly, by opening the oven and cooling to room temperature, helps keep the filling from cracking.

Apple Pie

Prep Time: 50 Minutes • Start to Finish: 1 Hour 50 Minutes • 8 servings

CRUST

- ¾ **cup potato starch flour**
- ½ **cup tapioca flour**
- ½ **cup white rice flour**
- ¼ **cup garbanzo and fava flour**
- ¼ **cup sweet white sorghum flour**
- 1 **tablespoon sugar**
- ½ **teaspoon salt**
- 1 **egg**
- ¾ **cup canola oil**
- ¼ **cup water**
- ½ **teaspoon apple cider vinegar**
- 2 **teaspoons xanthan gum**
- 1 **teaspoon guar gum**
- ⅓ **cup chopped walnuts**
- ¼ **cup sugar**

FILLING

- 5 **cups chopped peeled apples (5 medium)**
- ½ **cup sugar**
- ¼ **cup plus 2 tablespoons water**
- ⅛ **teaspoon salt**
- 1 **teaspoon ground cinnamon**
- ⅛ **teaspoon ground nutmeg, if desired**
- 2 **tablespoons cornstarch**

1 Heat oven to 350°F. Spray bottom and sides of 9-inch glass pie plate with cooking spray (without flour). In small bowl, stir together all flours, 1 tablespoon sugar and ½ teaspoon salt; set aside.

2 In food processor, place egg, oil, ¼ cup water, the vinegar and both gums. Process 2 minutes. Add flour mixture; process 1 minute or until well mixed. Remove dough from food processor.

3 Place 1 cup of dough in medium bowl. Stir in walnuts and ¼ cup sugar; set aside. Press remaining dough (about 2 cups) in bottom and up side of pie plate.

4 In 3-quart saucepan, place apples, ½ cup sugar, ¼ cup water, ⅛ teaspoon salt, the cinnamon and nutmeg. Heat to boiling over high heat. Reduce heat to medium-low; cook 10 minutes, stirring occasionally.

5 In small bowl, mix cornstarch and 2 tablespoons water until smooth. Add to apple mixture; cook and stir about 1 minute or until mixture thickens. Pour filling into crust. Crumble walnut dough evenly over filling.

6 Bake 55 to 60 minutes or until crust is medium brown and filling is bubbly. Cool pie before serving.

1 Serving: Calories 510 (Calories from Fat 220); Total Fat 25g (Saturated Fat 2g; Trans Fat 0g); Cholesterol 25mg; Sodium 200mg; Total Carbohydrate 68g (Dietary Fiber 3g); Protein 3g **% Daily Value:** Vitamin A 0%; Vitamin C 2%; Calcium 0%; Iron 4% **Exchanges:** ½ Starch, 2 Fruit, 2 Other Carbohydrate, 5 Fat **Carbohydrate Choices:** 4½

Contributed by Jean Duane Alternative Cook http://www.alternativecook.com

> **Cooking the apples** on the stovetop and thickening with cornstarch before adding the filling to the pie ensures that the apples are soft and the filling is evenly thickened.

Blueberry Pie with Cornmeal Crust

Prep Time: 45 Minutes • Start to Finish: 4 Hours • 8 servings

CRUST

- 1 **cup white rice flour**
- ½ **cup tapioca flour**
- ¼ **cup potato starch flour**
- ½ **cup cornmeal**
- 2 **tablespoons sugar**
- 1 **teaspoon xanthan gum**
- ½ **teaspoon salt**
- ¼ **teaspoon pumpkin pie spice**
- ½ **cup very cold butter, cut into ½-inch pieces**
- ¼ **cup very cold shortening, cut into ½-inch pieces**
- ¼ **cup ice water**

FILLING

- 5 **cups fresh blueberries (about 1½ lb)**
- ½ **cup sugar**
- ⅓ **cup cornstarch**
- 1 **jar (12 oz) gluten-free blueberry preserves**
- ¼ **cup butter, cut into small pieces**
- 1 **teaspoon grated lemon peel**
- 1 **tablespoon fresh lemon juice**
- ⅛ **teaspoon salt**
- 1 **egg, separated**
- 1 **tablespoon milk**
- 1 **tablespoon sugar**

Want an all-butter crust?
Go ahead and eliminate the shortening and add ¼ cup more butter. Feel free to use your favorite berry preserves or jam instead of blueberry.

1 In food processor, place flours, cornmeal, 2 tablespoons sugar, the xanthan gum, ½ teaspoon salt and the pumpkin pie spice. Cover; pulse, using quick on-and-off motions, until blended. Add ½ cup butter and the shortening. Cover; pulse until coarse crumbs form, about 5 seconds. Add water; pulse just until dough comes together. Divide dough in half; flatten each into a disk. Wrap in plastic wrap; refrigerate until firm.

2 In large bowl, toss blueberries, ½ cup sugar, the cornstarch, preserves, ¼ cup butter, lemon peel, lemon juice and ⅛ teaspoon salt; set aside.

3 Line cookie sheet with foil; place on lower oven rack to catch any drips. Heat oven to 375°F. Unwrap 1 dough disk (keep remaining dough refrigerated until ready to use). Between 2 sheets of cooking parchment paper generously sprinkled with rice flour, roll dough into 12-inch round about ¼ inch thick. Carefully peel off top piece of parchment paper; replace paper and turn round over. Peel off parchment paper from second side of dough and discard.

4 Place upside-down 9-inch glass pie plate on dough round. Turn plate with dough over; remove parchment paper and discard. Pat dough into plate, pressing together any cracks or tears. In small bowl, beat egg white. Brush over dough. Spoon filling into crust-lined plate.

5 Unwrap second dough disk. Between 2 sheets of cooking parchment paper generously sprinkled with rice flour, roll dough into 12-inch round about ¼ inch thick. Carefully peel off top piece of parchment paper; invert dough onto filling. Peel off parchment paper from second side of dough and discard. Using sharp knife, trim crusts even with edge of plate; crimp edge with fork to seal. Cut vents in top crust. In small bowl, beat egg yolk and milk. Brush over dough. Sprinkle with 1 tablespoon sugar.

6 Bake 1 hour to 1 hour 10 minutes or until crust is golden and filling is bubbly. Cool completely on cooling rack, about 2 hours.

1 Serving: Calories 640 (Calories from Fat 230); Total Fat 25g (Saturated Fat 13g; Trans Fat 2g); Cholesterol 70mg; Sodium 210mg; Total Carbohydrate 100g (Dietary Fiber 4g); Protein 4g **% Daily Value:** Vitamin A 15%; Vitamin C 10%; Calcium 4%; Iron 6% **Exchanges:** 2 Starch, ½ Fruit, 4 Other Carbohydrate, 5 Fat **Carbohydrate Choices:** 6½

Contributed by Silvana Nardone Silvana's Kitchen http://silvanaskitchen.com

Luscious Meringue Lemon Pie

Prep Time: 45 Minutes • Start to Finish: 4 Hours • 8 servings

CRUST

4 cups Rice Chex® cereal

2 tablespoons potato starch flour

¼ cup sunflower or canola oil or melted ghee

2 tablespoons packed brown sugar

⅛ teaspoon salt

1 whole egg

FILLING

4 egg yolks

1 cup water

1 cup granulated sugar

⅓ cup lemon juice

6 tablespoons cornstarch

1 tablespoon melted ghee or sunflower oil

MERINGUE

4 egg whites

½ cup granulated sugar

1 Heat oven to 350°F. Spray 9-inch glass pie plate with cooking spray (without flour).

2 In food processor, place cereal. Cover; process until crushed. Add remaining crust ingredients. Cover; process until crumbly. Press mixture into pie plate, starting in center and pressing up side. Bake 15 minutes or until golden brown. Cool completely on cooling rack.

3 In 3-quart saucepan, beat egg yolks, water, 1 cup granulated sugar, the lemon juice and cornstarch with whisk until well blended. Cook on high heat, stirring constantly with whisk until thickened. Remove from heat; stir in ghee until incorporated. Pour filling into crust.

4 In medium bowl, beat egg whites with electric mixer on high speed until soft peaks form. Gradually add ½ cup granulated sugar, 1 tablespoon at a time, beating until stiff peaks form. Spoon meringue onto hot filling, spreading to edges to seal. Bake 15 minutes or until meringue is golden brown. Cool on cooling rack 30 minutes. Refrigerate 2 to 3 hours before serving.

1 Serving: Calories 370 (Calories from Fat 100); Total Fat 11g (Saturated Fat 2.5g; Trans Fat 0g); Cholesterol 135mg; Sodium 210mg; Total Carbohydrate 61g (Dietary Fiber 0g); Protein 5g **% Daily Value:** Vitamin A 10%; Vitamin C 6%; Calcium 8%; Iron 25% **Exchanges:** 1½ Starch, 2½ Other Carbohydrate, 2 Fat **Carbohydrate Choices:** 4

Contributed by Jean Duane Alternative Cook http://www.alternativecook.com

> **Use a glass or metal bowl** when beating eggs for a meringue. Plastic bowls have just enough oil to ruin meringue.

Easy Strawberry Pie

Prep Time: 15 Minutes • Start to Finish: 3 Hours • 8 servings

CRUST

6 **cups Rice Chex® cereal**

⅓ **cup sunflower or canola oil or melted ghee**

3 **tablespoons potato starch flour**

¼ **cup sugar**

¼ **teaspoon salt**

1 **egg**

FILLING

2 **lb fresh strawberries, sliced (about 5 cups)**

1 **container (13.5 oz) gluten-free glaze for strawberries**

1 Heat oven to 350°F. Spray 10-inch glass pie plate with cooking spray (without flour).

2 In food processor, place cereal. Cover; process until crushed. Add remaining crust ingredients. Cover; process until incorporated. Press mixture into pie plate, starting in center and pressing up side. Bake 15 minutes or until golden brown. Cool completely on cooling rack.

3 In large bowl, stir strawberries and glaze until covered. Spread filling into crust. Refrigerate 2 hours before serving.

1 Serving: Calories 250 (Calories from Fat 90); Total Fat 10g (Saturated Fat 1g; Trans Fat 0g); Cholesterol 25mg; Sodium 280mg; Total Carbohydrate 37g (Dietary Fiber 2g); Protein 3g **% Daily Value:** Vitamin A 8%; Vitamin C 60%; Calcium 10%; Iron 40% **Exchanges:** 1 Starch, 1½ Other Carbohydrate, 2 Fat **Carbohydrate Choices:** 2½

Contributed by Jean Duane Alternative Cook http://www.alternativecook.com

Garnish slices with a dollop of whipped cream, if desired. Soy whipped cream is available for those avoiding dairy products.

Crème de Menthe Brownie Pie

Prep Time: 30 Minutes • Start to Finish: 3 Hours • 8 servings

CRUST

1 **box Betty Crocker® Gluten Free brownie mix**

¼ **cup butter, melted**

2 **whole eggs**

FILLING

1 **cup almond milk**

1 **teaspoon unflavored gelatin**

⅓ **cup sugar**

2 **egg yolks**

2 **tablespoons cornstarch**

1 **tablespoon crème de menthe**

1 **tablespoon white crème de cacao**

⅛ **teaspoon salt**

4 **oz (half of 8-oz container) frozen whipped topping, thawed**

½ **cup miniature semisweet chocolate chips**

1 Heat oven to 350°F (325°F for dark or nonstick pan). Spray bottom only of 8- or 9-inch square pan with cooking spray (without flour).

2 In medium bowl, stir brownie mix, butter and eggs until well blended (batter will be thick). Spread in pan.

3 Bake 8-inch pan 28 to 31 minutes, 9-inch pan 26 to 30 minutes, or until toothpick inserted 2 inches from side of pan comes out almost clean. Cool completely in pan on cooling rack, about 1 hour.

4 Meanwhile, in 3-quart saucepan, mix all filling ingredients except whipped topping and chocolate chips. Cook over medium heat, stirring constantly with whisk until mixture starts to boil; boil and stir 1 minute longer until thickened. Remove from heat. Refrigerate in pan about 30 minutes until cool.

5 Cut brownies into very small pieces, about 36. In 9-inch glass pie plate, press brownie pieces together on bottom and up side of plate. Stir whipped topping and chocolate chips into filling. Spoon into brownie crust and spread evenly. Refrigerate 1 hour before serving.

1 Serving: Calories 480 (Calories from Fat 170); Total Fat 19g (Saturated Fat 11g; Trans Fat 0g); Cholesterol 120mg; Sodium 240mg; Total Carbohydrate 70g (Dietary Fiber 3g); Protein 5g **% Daily Value:** Vitamin A 8%; Vitamin C 0%; Calcium 6%; Iron 15% **Exchanges:** 1½ Starch, 3½ Other Carbohydrate, 3½ Fat **Carbohydrate Choices:** 4½

To cut calories and fat in this decadent dessert, use fat-free whipped topping and fewer chocolate chips.

Impossibly Easy Peach and Raspberry Pie

Prep Time: 15 Minutes • Start to Finish: 1 Hour 50 Minutes • 8 servings

FILLING

- **1 bag (12 oz) frozen sliced peaches, thawed, patted dry and cut into ¾-inch pieces**
- **½ teaspoon ground cinnamon**
- **¼ teaspoon ground nutmeg**
- **1 cup fresh raspberries**
- **½ cup Bisquick® Gluten Free mix**
- **⅓ cup whipping cream**
- **⅔ cup sugar**
- **2 eggs, beaten**
- **1 teaspoon pure almond extract**

TOPPING

- **2 tablespoons Bisquick® Gluten Free mix**
- **¼ cup sugar**
- **2 tablespoons cold butter**
- **½ cup slivered almonds**

1 Heat oven to 350°F. Spray 9-inch glass pie plate with cooking spray (without flour).

2 In medium bowl, stir peaches, cinnamon and nutmeg. Spoon peaches into pie plate; sprinkle with raspberries. In small bowl, stir ½ cup Bisquick mix, the whipping cream, ⅔ cup sugar, the eggs and almond extract until smooth. Pour mixture over fruit. Bake 10 minutes.

3 Meanwhile, in another small bowl, stir 2 tablespoons Bisquick mix and ¼ cup sugar. Cut in butter, with pastry blender or fork, until crumbly. Stir in almonds. Sprinkle topping over pie.

4 Return pie to oven; bake an additional 30 to 35 minutes or until knife inserted in center comes out clean and topping is golden brown. Cool on cooling rack at least 1 hour before serving. Store covered in refrigerator.

1 Serving: Calories 230 (Calories from Fat 90); Total Fat 10g (Saturated Fat 4.5g; Trans Fat 0g); Cholesterol 70mg; Sodium 150mg; Total Carbohydrate 29g (Dietary Fiber 2g); Protein 4g **% Daily Value:** Vitamin A 10%; Vitamin C 35%; Calcium 4%; Iron 4% **Exchanges:** 1 Starch, 1 Other Carbohydrate, 2 Fat **Carbohydrate Choices:** 2

> **Peaches** are a good source of vitamin A, which promotes healthy vision.

Impossibly Easy French Apple Pie

Prep Time: 25 Minutes • Start to Finish: 1 Hour 15 Minutes • 6 servings

FILLING

- 3 cups thinly sliced peeled apples (3 medium)
- 1 teaspoon ground cinnamon
- ¼ teaspoon ground nutmeg
- ½ cup Bisquick® Gluten Free mix
- ½ cup granulated sugar
- ½ cup milk
- 2 tablespoons butter or margarine, melted
- 3 eggs

STREUSEL

- ⅓ cup Bisquick® Gluten Free mix
- ⅓ cup chopped walnuts
- ¼ cup packed brown sugar
- 3 tablespoons cold butter or margarine

1 Heat oven to 325°F. Spray 9-inch glass pie plate with cooking spray (without flour). In medium bowl, mix apples, cinnamon and nutmeg; place in pie plate.

2 In medium bowl, stir remaining filling ingredients until well blended. Pour over apple mixture in pie plate. In small bowl, mix all streusel ingredients with fork until crumbly; sprinkle over filling.

3 Bake 45 to 50 minutes or until knife inserted in center comes out clean. Store in refrigerator. Cool 5 minutes.

1 Serving: Calories 380 (Calories from Fat 150); Total Fat 17g (Saturated Fat 8g; Trans Fat 0g); Cholesterol 135mg; Sodium 300mg; Total Carbohydrate 49g (Dietary Fiber 2g); Protein 6g **% Daily Value:** Vitamin A 10%; Vitamin C 0%; Calcium 8%; Iron 4% **Exchanges:** 1½ Starch, 2 Other Carbohydrate, 3 Fat **Carbohydrate Choices:** 3

> **The best varieties of apples** to use in baked goods are Braeburn, Fuji, Gala, Golden Delicious, Granny Smith, Greening, Haralson, Jonagold, Newton Peppin, Prairie Spy and San Rose.

Impossibly Easy Coconut Pie

Prep Time: 10 Minutes • **Start to Finish:** 1 Hour • 8 servings

3 eggs
1¾ cups milk
¼ cup butter, melted
1½ teaspoons pure vanilla
1 cup flaked or shredded coconut
¾ cup sugar
½ cup Bisquick® Gluten Free mix

1 Heat oven to 350°F. Grease 9-inch glass pie plate with shortening or cooking spray (without flour). In large bowl, stir together all ingredients until blended. Pour into pie plate.

2 Bake 45 to 50 minutes or until golden brown and knife inserted in the center comes out clean. Store any remaining pie covered in refrigerator. Cool 5 minutes.

1 Serving: Calories 260 (Calories from Fat 110); Total Fat 13g (Saturated Fat 8g; Trans Fat 0g); Cholesterol 100mg; Sodium 180mg; Total Carbohydrate 32g (Dietary Fiber 0g); Protein 4g **% Daily Value:** Vitamin A 8%; Vitamin C 0%; Calcium 8%; Iron 2% **Exchanges:** ½ Starch, 1½ Other Carbohydrate, 2½ Fat **Carbohydrate Choices:** 2

Read coconut packages closely and you'll notice that there are two types available: flaked and shredded. Flaked coconut is cut into small pieces and is drier than shredded coconut. Either type works well in most recipes, but using shredded results in a more moist and chewy finished product.

Celebration Trifle

Prep Time: 30 Minutes • Start to Finish: 3 Hours 30 Minutes • 10 servings

1 box Betty Crocker® Gluten Free yellow cake mix

Water, butter, pure vanilla and eggs as called for on cake mix box

½ cup sugar

¼ cup cornstarch

2 cups milk

2 eggs, lightly beaten

2 tablespoons butter

1 teaspoon pure vanilla

¾ cup whipping cream

¼ cup raspberry-flavored liqueur, brandy or thawed apple juice concentrate

2 cups raspberries or sliced strawberries

2 mangoes, peeled, cut-up

½ cup flaked or shredded coconut, toasted

1 Heat oven to 350°F (or 325°F for dark or nonstick pan). Grease bottom only of 8-inch or 9-inch square pan with shortening. Make and bake cake as directed on box using water, butter, vanilla and eggs. Run knife around sides of pan to loosen cake. Cool 1 hour.

2 Meanwhile, in heavy 2-quart heavy saucepan, stir together sugar and cornstarch; stir in milk. Cook and stir over medium heat until thickened and bubbly. In medium bowl, beat eggs with whisk just until blended. Gradually stir 1 cup hot milk mixture into egg mixture, whisking constantly, until combined. Pour milk and egg mixture back into saucepan. Return to medium heat. Cook, stirring constantly, 1 to 2 minutes longer, or until thick and bubbly. Remove from heat. Stir in butter and vanilla. Press plastic wrap on filling to prevent a tough layer from forming on top. Refrigerate at least 1 hour.

3 In medium bowl, beat whipping cream until stiff peaks form. Fold whipped cream into pudding mixture until combined.

4 Cut cake into 1-inch pieces. In large bowl or trifle bowl, place half of the cake pieces. Brush or sprinkle half the liqueur over cake. Spoon half of the berries, half of the mangoes and half of the coconut over cake. Spread half of the pudding mixture over coconut. Repeat with remaining cake, liqueur, berries, mangoes and coconut. Cover; refrigerate at least 1 hour before serving. If desired, garnish with additional fruit and coconut. Store any remaining trifle covered in refrigerator.

1 Serving: Calories 480 (Calories from Fat 200); Total Fat 23g (Saturated Fat 14g; Trans Fat 0.5g); Cholesterol 160mg; Sodium 380mg; Total Carbohydrate 58g (Dietary Fiber 2g); Protein 7g **% Daily Value:** Vitamin A 20%; Vitamin C 30%; Calcium 10%; Iron 4% **Exchanges:** 2 Starch, 1 Fruit, 1 Other Carbohydrate, 4½ Fat **Carbohydrate Choices:** 4

Select a clear liqueur to keep the color of the cake from turning purple.

Chocolate Chip Cookie Ice Cream Pie

Prep Time: 15 Minutes • Start to Finish: 3 Hours • 8 servings

1 box Betty Crocker® Gluten Free chocolate chip cookie mix

½ cup butter, softened

1 teaspoon pure vanilla

1 egg, beaten

1 tablespoon unsweetened baking cocoa

1½ quarts gluten-free vanilla ice cream

½ cup gluten-free chocolate fudge topping

1 Heat oven to 350°F. In medium bowl, stir cookie mix, butter, vanilla and egg until soft dough forms. Divide dough in half (about 2 cups in each half). With half of the dough, shape, bake and cool cookies as directed on box. Reserve for another use.

2 Meanwhile, stir cocoa into remaining half of dough. Crumble dough onto cookie sheet with sides. Bake 8 to 10 minutes until dough is baked through and just starting to turn light brown. Cool 5 minutes; toss with spatula to make crumbs.

3 In ungreased 9-inch glass pie plate, press 1 cup of the cookie crumbs. Place small scoops of ice cream in single layer over crust; sprinkle with ¾ cup of the crumbs. Top with remaining ice cream and crumbs. Cover; freeze at least 2 hours.

4 In small microwavable bowl, microwave chocolate fudge topping on High 10 to 15 seconds. Drizzle topping over pie just before serving.

1 Serving: Calories 670 (Calories from Fat 270); Total Fat 30g (Saturated Fat 17g; Trans Fat 1g); Cholesterol 100mg; Sodium 550mg; Total Carbohydrate 93g (Dietary Fiber 1g); Protein 7g **% Daily Value:** Vitamin A 15%; Vitamin C 0%; Calcium 20%; Iron 2% **Exchanges:** 2 Starch, 4 Other Carbohydrate, 6 Fat **Carbohydrate Choices:** 6

For extra chocolate impact, drizzle ¼ cup gluten-free chocolate fudge topping over crumbs in bottom of pie plate before topping with ice cream as directed.

Apple-Cranberry Crisp

Prep Time: 15 Minutes • Start to Finish: 55 Minutes • 6 servings

FILLING

- **5 cups chopped peeled apples (5 medium)**
- **½ cup sweetened dried cranberries**
- **¼ cup packed brown sugar**
- **1 teaspoon ground cinnamon**
- **⅛ teaspoon ground nutmeg**
- **1 teaspoon grated lemon peel or ½ teaspoon dried lemon peel**
- **1 teaspoon pure vanilla**
- **¾ cup water**
- **¼ cup cornstarch**
- **¼ teaspoon salt**

TOPPING

- **1 cup gluten-free old-fashioned oats**
- **1 cup Rice Chex® cereal, crushed**
- **½ cup chopped walnuts**
- **¼ cup slivered almonds**
- **½ cup packed brown sugar**
- **½ cup melted ghee**
- **½ teaspoon salt**

1 Heat oven to 350°F. Spray bottom and sides of 8-inch square (2-quart) glass baking dish with cooking spray (without flour).

2 In large microwaveable bowl, microwave apples on High 5 minutes. Remove from microwave. Stir in dried cranberries, ¼ cup brown sugar, the cinnamon, nutmeg, lemon peel and vanilla.

3 In small bowl, stir water, cornstarch and ¼ teaspoon salt until dissolved. Stir into apple mixture. Spoon mixture into baking dish.

4 In medium bowl, mix topping ingredients. Spread evenly over apple mixture.

5 Bake 20 to 25 minutes or until bubbly. Cool 15 minutes. Serve warm.

1 Serving: Calories 580 (Calories from Fat 270); Total Fat 30g (Saturated Fat 13g; Trans Fat 0g); Cholesterol 30mg; Sodium 350mg; Total Carbohydrate 70g (Dietary Fiber 6g); Protein 6g **% Daily Value:** Vitamin A 15%; Vitamin C 4%; Calcium 8%; Iron 20% **Exchanges:** 1 Starch, ½ Fruit, 3 Other Carbohydrate, ½ Very Lean Meat, 6 Fat **Carbohydrate Choices:** 4½

Contributed by Jean Duane Alternative Cook http://www.alternativecook.com

Even though gluten-free oats are often available, check with your doctor about whether eating gluten-free oats is recommended for you if you're on a gluten-free diet. Instead you can easily substitute any "flaked grain" for the oats such as quinoa flakes, buckwheat or rice flakes, or substitute your favorite gluten-free breakfast cereal.

Double Peanut Butter Cookies

Prep Time: 1 Hour 30 Minutes • Start to Finish: 1 Hour 30 Minutes • 2 dozen cookies

COOKIES

- 1 **cup brown rice flour**
- 1 **cup sweet white sorghum flour**
- ¼ **cup white rice flour**
- ¼ **cup tapioca flour**
- ¼ **cup garbanzo and fava flour**
- ¼ **cup potato starch flour**
- 1½ **teaspoons xanthan gum**
- 2 **teaspoons gluten-free baking powder**
- ½ **teaspoon salt**
- ½ **cup crunchy peanut butter**
- ¼ **cup sunflower or canola oil**
- 2 **eggs**
- 1 **cup packed brown sugar**
- ¼ **cup almond milk, soymilk or regular milk**
- 2 **teaspoons pure vanilla**

FILLING

- ½ **cup crunchy peanut butter**
- ½ **cup gluten-free powdered sugar**

TOPPING

- 2 **tablespoons granulated sugar**

1 Heat oven to 350°F. Line cookie sheet with cooking parchment paper; spray paper with cooking spray (without flour).

2 In small bowl, mix flours, xanthan gum, baking powder and salt with whisk; set aside. In medium bowl, beat ½ cup peanut butter, the oil, eggs, brown sugar, milk and vanilla with electric mixer on medium speed until well blended. Gradually add flour mixture, beating on low speed until blended.

3 In small bowl, mix ½ cup peanut butter and the powdered sugar until fully incorporated; form into ball. Divide filling into 24 pieces and shape into balls; set aside.

4 Divide cookie dough into 24 pieces and shape into balls. Flatten each ball into 2½-inch round; place 1 filling ball on each dough round and shape dough around filling, covering completely. In small bowl, place granulated sugar. Roll each ball in sugar and place on cookie sheet. Flatten in crisscross pattern with fork.

5 Bake 9 to 11 minutes or until set. Cool 5 minutes; remove from cookie sheet to cooling rack.

1 Serving: Calories 210 (Calories from Fat 80); Total Fat 9g (Saturated Fat 1.5g; Trans Fat 0g); Cholesterol 20mg; Sodium 150mg; Total Carbohydrate 29g (Dietary Fiber 2g); Protein 5g **% Daily Value:** Vitamin A 0%; Vitamin C 0%; Calcium 4%; Iron 4% **Exchanges:** 1 Starch, 1 Other Carbohydrate, 1½ Fat **Carbohydrate Choices:** 2

Contributed by Jean Duane Alternative Cook http://www.alternativecook.com

Peanut butter, made from ground peanuts, is a good source of protein and unsaturated fat—there's a double dose here. To make the cookie dough easier to handle when shaping into balls, and avoid flour, spray your hands with cooking spray without flour. Repeat when dough begins to stick to your hands.

Jean's Snickerdoodles

Prep Time: 45 Minutes • Start to Finish: 45 Minutes • 1½ dozen cookies

COOKIES

- ½ cup white rice flour
- ½ cup tapioca flour
- ½ cup sweet white sorghum flour
- ½ cup potato starch flour
- 2 teaspoons xanthan gum
- 1 teaspoon cream of tartar
- ¼ teaspoon gluten-free baking powder
- ¼ teaspoon salt
- 2 eggs
- ½ cup melted ghee
- ¾ cup sugar
- 2 teaspoons pure vanilla
- 1 teaspoon gluten-free vanilla bean paste, if desired

TOPPING

- 2 tablespoons sugar
- 1 teaspoon ground cinnamon

1 Heat oven to 350°F. Line cookie sheet with cooking parchment paper; spray paper with cooking spray (without flour).

2 In small bowl, mix flours, xanthan gum, cream of tartar, baking powder and salt with whisk; set aside. In medium bowl, beat eggs, ghee, ¾ cup sugar, the vanilla and vanilla bean paste. Gradually add flour mixture, beating until well blended.

3 In small bowl, mix 2 tablespoons sugar and the cinnamon. Drop dough by tablespoonfuls into topping and roll to coat. Place balls on cookie sheet; flatten slightly.

4 Bake 19 to 21 minutes or until golden brown. Cool 5 minutes; remove from cookie sheet to cooling rack.

1 Serving: Calories 160 (Calories from Fat 60); Total Fat 6g (Saturated Fat 3.5g; Trans Fat 0g); Cholesterol 40mg; Sodium 50mg; Total Carbohydrate 23g (Dietary Fiber 1g); Protein 1g **% Daily Value:** Vitamin A 4%; Vitamin C 0%; Calcium 0%; Iron 0% **Exchanges:** 1 Starch, ½ Other Carbohydrate, 1 Fat **Carbohydrate Choices:** 1½

Contributed by Jean Duane Alternative Cook http://www.alternativecook.com

Vanilla bean paste is made from ground vanilla beans mixed with vanilla extract. Adding it to these cookies boosts the vanilla flavor, but if you can't find it, they'll still taste great.

Ghee (clarified butter) is a butter substitute that does not contain the protein casein found in butter. It can be substituted one-for-one with oil, but not with butter. Butter contains water, which will throw off the ratios if used instead of oil or melted ghee. Ghee is found in the dairy section or baking aisle.

Slice 'n' Bake Oatmeal–Chocolate Chip Cookies

Prep Time: 35 Minutes • Start to Finish: 1 Hour 35 Minutes • 20 cookies

- 1 **cup gluten-free old-fashioned oats**
- ½ **cup gluten-free oat flour**
- ½ **cup brown rice flour**
- 2 **tablespoons tapioca flour**
- 1 **teaspoon gluten-free baking powder**
- ½ **teaspoon baking soda**
- 1 **teaspoon salt**
- ½ **cup butter, softened**
- ½ **cup packed brown sugar**
- ¼ **cup granulated sugar**
- 1 **egg**
- 1 **teaspoon pure vanilla**
- 1 **cup miniature semisweet chocolate chips**
- ½ **cup chopped walnuts**

1 In small bowl, mix oats, flours, baking powder, baking soda and salt with whisk; set aside. In large bowl, beat butter, brown sugar and granulated sugar with electric mixer on medium speed until fluffy. Beat in egg and vanilla. Gradually add oat mixture, beating on low speed just until combined. Stir in chocolate chips and nuts.

2 Shape dough into 16x1½x1½-inch log; wrap in plastic wrap. Refrigerate 1 hour or until firm.

3 Heat oven to 350°F. Unwrap dough. Using serrated knife, cut dough into ½-inch slices. Place 2 inches apart on ungreased cookie sheet.

4 Bake 9 to 11 minutes or just until edges are golden. Cool 2 minutes; remove from cookie sheet to cooling rack.

1 Serving: Calories 190 (Calories from Fat 90); Total Fat 10g (Saturated Fat 5g; Trans Fat 0g); Cholesterol 25mg; Sodium 180mg; Total Carbohydrate 22g (Dietary Fiber 1g); Protein 2g **% Daily Value:** Vitamin A 4%; Vitamin C 0%; Calcium 4%; Iron 4% **Exchanges:** ½ Starch, 1 Other Carbohydrate, 2 Fat **Carbohydrate Choices:** 1½

Contributed by Silvana Nardone Silvana's Kitchen http://silvanaskitchen.com

You can refrigerate the cookie dough log up to 1 week or freeze in resealable freezer plastic bag up to 2 months. If frozen, there's no need to thaw the dough before slicing and baking. And, instead of shaping the dough into a log and chilling it, you can simply drop the dough by rounded tablespoonfuls onto the cookie sheet and bake.

Nutty Chocolate–Chocolate Chip Cookies

Prep Time: 1 Hour 10 Minutes • Start to Finish: 1 Hour 10 Minutes • 2 dozen cookies

½ cup sweet white sorghum flour

½ cup tapioca flour

¼ cup white rice flour

¼ cup almond flour

¼ cup garbanzo and fava flour

½ cup unsweetened baking cocoa

1½ teaspoons xanthan gum

½ teaspoon salt

¼ teaspoon baking soda

1 egg

½ cup sunflower or canola oil

1 cup sugar

2 teaspoons pure vanilla

¼ cup almond milk, soymilk or regular milk

½ cup miniature semisweet chocolate chips

¼ cup chopped walnuts

2 tablespoons sugar

1 Heat oven to 350°F. Spray cookie sheet with cooking spray (without flour).

2 In small bowl, mix flours, cocoa, xanthan gum, salt and baking soda. In medium bowl, beat egg, oil, 1 cup sugar, the vanilla and milk with electric mixer on medium speed until well blended. Gradually add flour mixture, beating until blended. Stir in chocolate chips and nuts.

3 In small bowl, place 2 tablespoons sugar. Shape dough into 1½-inch balls; dip tops in sugar. Place on cookie sheet.

4 Bake 15 to 17 minutes or until set. Cool 5 minutes; remove from cookie sheet to cooling rack.

1 Cookie: Calories 150 (Calories from Fat 70); Total Fat 8g (Saturated Fat 1.5g; Trans Fat 0g); Cholesterol 10mg; Sodium 65mg; Total Carbohydrate 20g (Dietary Fiber 1g); Protein 1g **% Daily Value:** Vitamin A 0%; Vitamin C 0%; Calcium 0%; Iron 4% **Exchanges:** ½ Starch, 1 Other Carbohydrate, 1½ Fat **Carbohydrate Choices:** 1

Contributed by Jean Duane Alternative Cook http://www.alternativecook.com

Sorghum, a grass that is ground into flour for gluten-free baking, provides 4 grams of fiber per half cup. These cookies freeze well for a quick snack. For a cake-like cookie, eliminate the chocolate chips and nuts.

Snickerdoodles

Prep Time: 50 Minutes • Start to Finish: 50 Minutes • 2½ dozen cookies

2 eggs
1¼ cups sugar
¼ cup butter, softened
¼ cup shortening
2 cups Bisquick® Gluten Free mix
2 teaspoons ground cinnamon

1 Heat oven to 375°F. In large bowl, mix eggs, 1 cup of the sugar, the butter and shortening. Stir in Bisquick mix until dough forms.

2 In small bowl, mix remaining ¼ cup sugar and the cinnamon. Shape dough into 1¼-inch balls. (If dough feels too soft for shaping into balls, put dough in freezer for 10 to 15 minutes.) Roll balls in sugar-cinnamon mixture; place 2 inches apart on ungreased cookie sheets.

3 Bake 10 to 12 minutes or until set. Immediately remove from cookie sheets to cooling racks.

1 Cookie: Calories 100 (Calories from Fat 35); Total Fat 3.5g (Saturated Fat 1.5g; Trans Fat 0g); Cholesterol 20mg; Sodium 105mg; Total Carbohydrate 15g (Dietary Fiber 0g); Protein 1g **% Daily Value:** Vitamin A 0%; Vitamin C 0%; Calcium 0%; Iron 0% **Exchanges:** ½ Starch, ½ Other Carbohydrate, ½ Fat **Carbohydrate Choices:** 1

These rich cinnamon-sugar cookies make a great gift! Place a bag of them in a small basket along with packets of cappuccino or hot chocolate mix.

Sugar Cookies

Prep Time: 20 Minutes • Start to Finish: 2 Hours 25 Minutes • 20 cookies

1 cup sorghum flour

1 cup white rice flour

½ cup almond flour

½ cup potato starch flour

1 teaspoon cream of tartar

1 teaspoon baking soda

1 teaspoon gluten-free baking powder

1 teaspoon xanthan gum

½ teaspoon salt

1 cup granulated sugar

½ cup melted ghee or coconut oil

1 teaspoon pure vanilla

½ teaspoon lemon oil

2 eggs

2 tablespoons coarse sugar

1 In small bowl, stir together all flours, cream of tartar, baking soda, baking powder, xanthan gum and salt; set aside.

2 In medium bowl, beat remaining ingredients except coarse sugar with electric mixer on low speed 1 minute or until well blended. Add flour mixture; beat until blended. Shape dough into a ball. Wrap in plastic wrap; refrigerate at least 2 hours.

3 Heat oven to 350°F. Spray cookie sheets and rolling pin with cooking spray (without flour). On nonstick baking mat or cooking parchment paper sprayed with cooking spray, roll dough to ¼-inch thickness with rolling pin. Using 3- to 3½-inch cookie cutter, cut shapes from dough; place 1 to 1½ inches apart on cookie sheets. Sprinkle with coarse sugar.

4 Bake 10 to 15 minutes or until set and lightly browned on edges. Immediately remove from cookie sheets to cooling racks.

1 Cookie: Calories 190 (Calories from Fat 70); Total Fat 8g (Saturated Fat 5g; Trans Fat 0g); Cholesterol 20mg; Sodium 150mg; Total Carbohydrate 28g (Dietary Fiber 1g); Protein 2g **% Daily Value:** Vitamin A 0%; Vitamin C 0%; Calcium 2%; Iron 2% **Exchanges:** ½ Starch, 1½ Other Carbohydrate, 1½ Fat **Carbohydrate Choices:** 2

Contributed by Jean Duane Alternative Cook http://www.alternativecook.com

Nonstick baking mats are silicone baking surfaces. They are available at most cooking stores. Since they are woven with glass, only use plastic cookie cutters or a plastic knife.

The lemon oil adds a nice flavor to the sugar cookie. It is available at most kitchen or cookware stores.

Ranger Cookies

Prep Time: 45 Minutes • Start to Finish: 45 Minutes • 4 dozen cookies

½ cup creamy peanut butter

⅓ cup butter, softened

1 teaspoon pure vanilla

2 eggs, beaten

1 box Betty Crocker® Gluten Free chocolate chip cookie mix

2 cups Rice Chex® cereal, crushed

1 cup gluten-free candied-coated chocolate candies

1 Heat oven to 350°F. In large bowl, beat peanut butter, butter, vanilla and eggs with electric mixer on low speed until creamy. Add cookie mix, beating on low speed until blended. Stir in cereal and candies.

2 Onto ungreased cookie sheets, drop tablespoonfuls of dough about 1 inch apart; flatten slightly.

3 Bake 8 to 10 minutes or until light golden brown. Cool 1 minute; remove from cookie sheets to cooling racks. Store cooled cookies covered at room temperature.

1 Serving: Calories 100 (Calories from Fat 40); Total Fat 4.5g (Saturated Fat 2g; Trans Fat 0g); Cholesterol 15mg; Sodium 90mg; Total Carbohydrate 14g (Dietary Fiber 0g); Protein 1g **% Daily Value:** Vitamin A 0%; Vitamin C 0%; Calcium 0%; Iron 2% **Exchanges:** ½ Starch, ½ Other Carbohydrate, 1 Fat **Carbohydrate Choices:** 1

If you like warm cookies, bake only the amount of cookies you want. Refrigerate the remaining dough 2 to 3 days and bake fresh cookies as needed.

The gluten-free Chex® cereal provides at least 8 grams of whole grain per serving.

Chocolate Chip Sandwich Cookies

Prep Time: 15 Minutes • Start to Finish: 1 Hour • 22 sandwich cookies

COOKIES

- **1 box Betty Crocker® Gluten Free chocolate chip cookie mix**
- **½ cup butter, softened**
- **1 teaspoon pure vanilla**
- **1 egg, beaten**
- **¼ cup granulated sugar**

FILLING

- **1 cup semisweet chocolate chips (6 oz)**
- **½ cup creamy peanut butter**
- **⅓ cup whipping cream**
- **⅔ cup gluten-free powdered sugar**

1 Heat oven to 350°F. In medium bowl, stir cookie mix, butter, vanilla and egg until soft dough forms (dough will be crumbly).

2 In small bowl, place granulated sugar. Shape dough into 1-inch balls. Roll in sugar. On ungreased cookie sheets, place balls 2 inches apart. With bottom of smooth glass, press each ball to about ¼-inch thickness.

3 Bake 8 to 10 minutes or until edges are light golden brown. Cool 1 minute; remove from cookie sheets to cooling racks. Cool completely.

4 In medium bowl, place chocolate chips and peanut butter. In small microwavable bowl, microwave whipping cream on High 30 to 60 seconds. Pour cream over chips and peanut butter; stir until chips are melted. Stir in powdered sugar until smooth.

5 For each sandwich cookie, spread 1 tablespoon filling on bottom of 1 cookie; top with second cookie, bottom side down. Cool completely.

1 Serving: Calories 260 (Calories from Fat 110); Total Fat 13g (Saturated Fat 6g; Trans Fat 0g); Cholesterol 25mg; Sodium 180mg; Total Carbohydrate 33g (Dietary Fiber 0g); Protein 3g **% Daily Value:** Vitamin A 4%; Vitamin C 0%; Calcium 2%; Iron 2% **Exchanges:** ½ Starch, 1½ Other Carbohydrate, 2½ Fat **Carbohydrate Choices:** 2

Roll edges of cookies in finely chopped peanuts, if you like.

Lemon Wedding Cookies

Prep Time: 1 Hour 10 Minutes • Start to Finish: 1 Hour 10 Minutes • 3 dozen cookies

1 cup sweet white sorghum flour

½ cup white rice flour

½ cup tapioca flour

½ cup potato starch flour

¼ cup garbanzo and fava flour

1 teaspoon xanthan gum

½ teaspoon guar gum

1 teaspoon baking soda

½ teaspoon salt

1 cup melted ghee or sunflower or canola oil

1½ cups gluten-free powdered sugar

2 eggs

2 teaspoons pure vanilla

2 teaspoons grated lemon peel

1 cup chopped pecans

1 Heat oven to 325°F. Spray cookie sheet with cooking spray (without flour).

2 In small bowl, mix flours, xanthan gum, guar gum, baking soda and salt with whisk; set aside. In medium bowl, beat ghee, ½ cup of the powdered sugar, the eggs, vanilla and lemon peel with electric mixer on medium speed. Gradually add flour mixture, beating until blended. Stir in pecans.

3 Shape dough into 1¼-inch balls; place on cookie sheet. Bake 11 to 13 minutes or until set. Cool 5 minutes.

4 Meanwhile, place remaining 1 cup powdered sugar in large resealable food-storage plastic bag. Drop 1 cookie at a time into bag and gently coat with sugar. Remove from bag and place on cooling rack.

1 Cookie: Calories 140 (Calories from Fat 70); Total Fat 8g (Saturated Fat 4g; Trans Fat 0g); Cholesterol 25mg; Sodium 75mg; Total Carbohydrate 14g (Dietary Fiber 1g); Protein 1g **% Daily Value:** Vitamin A 4%; Vitamin C 0%; Calcium 0%; Iron 2% **Exchanges:** ½ Starch, ½ Other Carbohydrate, 1½ Fat **Carbohydrate Choices:** 1

Contributed by Jean Duane Alternative Cook http://www.alternativecook.com

As an option, double-coat these cookies with powdered sugar, once when hot and again when cool, giving the outside a lovely finish.

Pumpkin–Chocolate Chip Cookies

Prep Time: 30 Minutes • Start to Finish: 1 Hour • 3 dozen cookies

¾ cup canned pumpkin (not pumpkin pie mix)

¼ cup butter, softened

1 teaspoon pure vanilla

1 egg

1 box Betty Crocker® Gluten Free chocolate chip cookie mix

½ cup raisins, if desired

¼ teaspoon ground cinnamon

Gluten-free powdered sugar, if desired

1 Heat oven to 350°F. Grease cookie sheets with shortening. In large bowl, stir pumpkin, butter, vanilla and egg until blended. Stir in cookie mix, raisins and cinnamon until soft dough forms.

2 On cookie sheets, drop dough by rounded tablespoonfuls 2 inches apart.

3 Bake 10 to 12 minutes or until almost no indentation remains when lightly touched in center and edges are golden brown. Immediately remove from cookie sheets to cooling racks. Cool completely, about 15 minutes. Sprinkle with powdered sugar.

1 Cookie: Calories 80 (Calories from Fat 25); Total Fat 2.5g (Saturated Fat 1.5g; Trans Fat 0g); Cholesterol 10mg; Sodium 80mg; Total Carbohydrate 13g (Dietary Fiber 0g); Protein 0g **% Daily Value:** Vitamin A 15%; Vitamin C 0%; Calcium 0%; Iron 0% **Exchanges:** 1 Other Carbohydrate, ½ Fat **Carbohydrate Choices:** 1

Dried currants or cranberries can be substituted for the raisins.

No-Bake Honey-Peanut Butter Bars

Prep Time: 15 Minutes • Start to Finish: 1 Hour • 24 bars

6 cups Honey Nut Chex® cereal

½ cup honey-roasted peanuts

½ cup honey or light corn syrup

¼ cup sugar

½ cup creamy peanut butter

¼ cup dark chocolate chips

1 Butter 9-inch or 8-inch square pan. In large bowl, mix cereal and peanuts; set aside.

2 In 3-quart saucepan, heat honey and sugar just to boiling over medium heat, stirring constantly. Remove from heat; stir in peanut butter until smooth. Pour over cereal mixture in bowl; stir gently until evenly coated. Press firmly in pan. Cool 15 minutes.

3 In small microwavable bowl, microwave chocolate chips uncovered on High 30 to 60 seconds, stirring every 15 seconds, until melted and smooth. Drizzle over top of bars. Let stand at room temperature at least 30 minutes or until chocolate is set. For bars, cut into 4 rows by 6 rows. Store loosely covered at room temperature.

1 Bar: Calories 130 (Calories from Fat 45); Total Fat 5g (Saturated Fat 1g; Trans Fat 0g); Cholesterol 0mg; Sodium 115mg; Total Carbohydrate 20g (Dietary Fiber 1g); Protein 3g **% Daily Value:** Vitamin A 4%; Vitamin C 0%; Calcium 4%; Iron 20% **Exchanges:** 1 Starch, 1 Fat **Carbohydrate Choices:** 1

Cleanup is easy when you spray the measuring cup with cooking spray (without flour) before adding the honey. It will slip right out!

Peanut Butter Cookie Candy Bars

Prep Time: 30 Minutes • Start to Finish: 2 Hours 35 Minutes • 36 bars

COOKIE BASE

1 box Betty Crocker® Gluten Free chocolate chip cookie mix

Butter, pure vanilla and egg called for on cookie mix box

FILLING

⅓ cup light corn syrup

3 tablespoons butter, softened

3 tablespoons creamy peanut butter

1 tablespoon plus 1½ teaspoons water

1¼ teaspoons pure vanilla

Dash salt

3½ cups gluten-free powdered sugar

CARAMEL LAYER

1 bag (14 oz) gluten-free caramels, unwrapped

2 tablespoons water

1½ cups dry-roasted peanuts

TOPPING

1 bag (11.5 oz) milk chocolate chips (2 cups)

1 Heat oven to 350°F. Make cookie dough as directed on box, using butter, vanilla and egg. In ungreased 13x9-inch pan, press dough evenly. Bake 18 to 20 minutes or until light golden brown. Cool about 30 minutes.

2 In large bowl, beat all filling ingredients except powdered sugar with electric mixer on medium speed until creamy and smooth. Gradually beat in powdered sugar until well blended (filling will be thick). Press filling over cookie base.

3 In medium microwavable bowl, microwave caramels and 2 tablespoons water uncovered on High 2 to 4 minutes, stirring twice, until caramels are melted. Stir in peanuts. Spread evenly over filling. Refrigerate about 15 minutes or until caramel layer is firm.

4 In small microwavable bowl, microwave chocolate chips uncovered on High 1 to 2 minutes, stirring once, until melted. Spread evenly over caramel layer. Refrigerate about 1 hour or until chocolate is set. For bars, cut into 6 rows by 6 rows. Store covered at room temperature.

1 Bar: Calories 290 (Calories from Fat 110); Total Fat 12g (Saturated Fat 5g; Trans Fat 0g); Cholesterol 20mg; Sodium 140mg; Total Carbohydrate 42g (Dietary Fiber 1g); Protein 3g **% Daily Value:** Vitamin A 2%; Vitamin C 0%; Calcium 4%; Iron 2% **Exchanges:** ½ Starch, 2½ Other Carbohydrate, 2½ Fat **Carbohydrate Choices:** 3

Powdered sugar is usually gluten-free since it's blended with cornstarch to keep it fluffy. However, some manufacturers use wheat products instead of cornstarch, so always check the label when purchasing.

Chocolate Peanut Butter Cookie Pizza

Prep Time: 10 Minutes • Start to Finish: 1 Hour 35 Minutes • 16 servings

1 box Betty Crocker Gluten® Free chocolate chip cookie mix

2 tablespoons unsweetened baking cocoa

½ cup butter, softened

1 egg, beaten

1 cup peanut butter chips (6 oz)

1 cup miniature marshmallows

½ cup chopped peanuts

2 tablespoons gluten-free hot fudge topping, heated

1 Heat oven to 350°F. In large bowl, stir cookie mix, cocoa, butter and egg until soft dough forms (dough will be crumbly). Pat in ungreased 12-inch pizza pan.

2 Bake 15 minutes or until cookie is puffed and set. Sprinkle with peanut butter chips, marshmallows and peanuts. Drizzle with hot fudge topping.

3 Bake 5 to 7 minutes longer or until chips are melted and marshmallows are puffed. Cool completely, about 1 hour. Cut into wedges.

1 Serving: Calories 250 (Calories from Fat 100); Total Fat 11g (Saturated Fat 6g; Trans Fat 0g); Cholesterol 30mg; Sodium 210mg; Total Carbohydrate 34g (Dietary Fiber 0g); Protein 3g **% Daily Value:** Vitamin A 4%; Vitamin C 0%; Calcium 4%; Iron 2% **Exchanges:** 1 Starch, 1½ Other Carbohydrate, 2 Fat **Carbohydrate Choices:** 2

To get a perfect slice, use a thin-bladed sharp knife. Run the knife under hot water and wipe dry with a paper towel between cuts.

Feel free to use butterscotch or milk chocolate chips in place of the peanut butter chips.

Sweet 'n' Salty Peanut Bars

Prep Time: 20 Minutes • Start to Finish: 2 Hours 10 Minutes • 24 bars

1 box Betty Crocker® Gluten Free chocolate chip cookie mix

½ cup butter, softened

1 teaspoon pure vanilla

1 egg, beaten

24 gluten-free caramels, unwrapped

2 tablespoons butter

1 can (14 oz) sweetened condensed milk (not evaporated)

1 can (12 oz) salted cocktail peanuts, chopped

1 cup semisweet chocolate chips (6 oz)

1 Heat oven to 350°F. Spray bottom and sides of 13x9-inch pan with cooking spray (without flour).

2 In medium bowl, stir cookie mix, ½ cup butter, the vanilla and egg until soft dough forms. Press in pan. Bake 15 minutes or until set.

3 Meanwhile, in 1-quart saucepan, heat caramels, 2 tablespoons butter and the condensed milk over medium-low heat 5 to 10 minutes, stirring frequently, until caramels are melted. Remove from heat. Carefully pour filling over partially baked crust; spread evenly. Sprinkle with peanuts. Bake 15 to 18 minutes or until filling is bubbly.

4 In small resealable freezer plastic bag, place chocolate chips; seal bag. Microwave on High 1 minute, kneading bag every 15 seconds, until chocolate is melted and smooth. Cut tiny corner off bag; squeeze bag to drizzle chocolate over bars. Cool on cooling rack 1 hour. Refrigerate 15 to 30 minutes or until chocolate is set. Cut into 6 rows by 4 rows.

1 Serving: Calories 340 (Calories from Fat 150); Total Fat 16g (Saturated Fat 7g; Trans Fat 0g); Cholesterol 30mg; Sodium 220mg; Total Carbohydrate 42g (Dietary Fiber 1g); Protein 6g **% Daily Value:** Vitamin A 4%; Vitamin C 0%; Calcium 8%; Iron 2% **Exchanges:** 1½ Starch, 1½ Other Carbohydrate, 3 Fat **Carbohydrate Choices:** 3

In place of the peanuts, use a 12-oz can of mixed nuts.

Peanut Butter-and-Jam Cookie Bars

Prep Time: 25 Minutes • Start to Finish: 2 Hours 25 Minutes • 24 bars

1¼ cups gluten-free old-fashioned oats

½ cup white rice flour

½ cup almond flour

¼ cup gluten-free oat flour

¼ cup tapioca flour

1 teaspoon gluten-free baking powder

½ teaspoon baking soda

1 cup coarsely chopped salted peanuts

½ cup butter, softened

½ cup sugar

½ cup creamy peanut butter

2 eggs

1 jar (12 oz) gluten-free grape jam

1 Heat oven to 350°F. Spray 13x9-inch pan with cooking spray (without flour).

2 In medium bowl, mix oats, flours, baking powder, baking soda and ¾ cup of the peanuts with whisk; set aside. In large bowl, beat butter, sugar and peanut butter with electric mixer on medium speed until blended. Beat in eggs. Gradually add oat mixture, beating on low just until combined.

3 Press two-thirds (about 3½ cups) of the dough in pan. Spread jam over crust. Drop heaping spoonfuls of remaining dough over jam. Sprinkle with remaining ¼ cup peanuts.

4 Bake 25 to 30 minutes or until set and golden brown. Cool in pan on cooling rack 1 hour. Refrigerate 30 minutes. Cut into 6 rows by 4 rows. Store in refrigerator.

1 Serving: Calories 220 (Calories from Fat 100); Total Fat 12g (Saturated Fat 3.5g; Trans Fat 0g); Cholesterol 30mg; Sodium 130mg; Total Carbohydrate 24g (Dietary Fiber 2g); Protein 5g **% Daily Value:** Vitamin A 2%; Vitamin C 0%; Calcium 4%; Iron 4% **Exchanges:** 1 Starch, ½ Other Carbohydrate, 2½ Fat **Carbohydrate Choices:** 1½

Contributed by Silvana Nardone Silvana's Kitchen http://silvanaskitchen.com

Substitute almond butter for the peanut butter and salted almonds for the peanuts, if you like, and use your family's favorite jam in place of the grape jam.

Oatmeal Caramel Bars

Prep Time: 10 Minutes • Start to Finish: 2 Hours 40 Minutes • 20 bars

1 box Betty Crocker® Gluten Free chocolate chip cookie mix

½ cup butter, softened

1 egg, beaten

1 teaspoon pure vanilla

2 cups gluten-free old-fashioned oats

1 bag (14 oz) gluten-free caramels, unwrapped

⅓ cup milk

1 Heat oven to 350°F. Spray 9-inch square pan with cooking spray (without flour).

2 In large bowl, stir cookie mix, butter, egg, vanilla and oats until crumbly. Press half of the mixture in pan. Reserve remaining crumb mixture for topping. Bake 10 minutes.

3 Meanwhile, in medium microwavable bowl, microwave caramels and milk uncovered on High 3 minutes, stirring after each minute, until caramels are melted. Stir until smooth. Pour caramel mixture over partially baked crust. Sprinkle with reserved crumb mixture; pat lightly.

4 Bake 15 to 18 minutes until lightly browned. Cool completely in pan on cooling rack, about 2 hours. Cut into 5 rows by 4 rows.

1 Serving: Calories 270 (Calories from Fat 80); Total Fat 9g (Saturated Fat 4.5g; Trans Fat 0g); Cholesterol 25mg; Sodium 210mg; Total Carbohydrate 44g (Dietary Fiber 0g); Protein 3g **% Daily Value:** Vitamin A 4%; Vitamin C 0%; Calcium 6%; Iron 2% **Exchanges:** 1½ Starch, 1½ Other Carbohydrate, 1½ Fat **Carbohydrate Choices:** 3

For easy removal and cutting, line the pan with foil, leaving 1 inch of foil overhanging at 2 opposite sides of pan; spray as directed. When cooled, use the foil to lift the bars out of the pan and place on a cutting board.

When using cooking spray, make sure it is gluten-free. Some cooking sprays are for baking and contain flour.

Ooey-Gooey Rocky Road Bars

Prep Time: 10 Minutes • Start to Finish: 1 Hour 25 Minutes • 24 bars

½ cup butter, softened

1 teaspoon pure vanilla

1 egg

1 box Betty Crocker® Gluten Free chocolate chip cookie mix

2 cups semisweet chocolate chips

½ cup chopped toasted pecans

3 cups miniature marshmallows

1 Heat oven to 350°F. Spray bottom only of 13x9-inch pan with cooking spray (without flour). In large bowl, mix butter, vanilla and egg until blended. Stir in cookie mix until soft dough forms. Press dough evenly in pan.

2 Bake 20 to 25 minutes or until top is golden brown and center puffs slightly. Immediately sprinkle chocolate chips over crust. Let stand 3 to 5 minutes or until chocolate begins to melt. Gently spread chocolate evenly over crust.

3 Set oven control to broil. Sprinkle nuts and marshmallows over melted chocolate. Broil with top 5 to 6 inches from heat 20 to 30 seconds or until marshmallows are toasted. (Watch closely; marshmallows will brown quickly.) Cool 30 to 45 minutes on cooling rack to serve warm or cool completely, about 2 hours. For bars, cut into 6 rows by 4 rows. Store tightly covered.

1 Bar: Calories 250 (Calories from Fat 100); Total Fat 12g (Saturated Fat 6g; Trans Fat 0g); Cholesterol 20mg; Sodium 140mg; Total Carbohydrate 33g (Dietary Fiber 1g); Protein 2g **% Daily Value:** Vitamin A 2%; Vitamin C 0%; Calcium 2%; Iron 4% **Exchanges:** ½ Starch, 1½ Other Carbohydrate, 2½ Fat **Carbohydrate Choices:** 2

These bars can be served warm or cool. Warm bars are very yummy, but are definitely ooey-gooey, so we recommend serving them on a little plate with a fork.

Peanut Butter–Chocolate Chip Bars with Chocolate Frosting

Prep Time: 15 Minutes • Start to Finish: 1 Hour 40 Minutes • 16 bars

1 box Betty Crocker® Gluten Free chocolate chip cookie mix

⅓ cup butter, softened

⅓ cup peanut butter

1 teaspoon pure vanilla

1 egg

1 cup Betty Crocker® Rich & Creamy chocolate frosting

1 Heat oven to 350°F (or 325°F for dark or nonstick pan). Grease bottom only of 8-inch or 9-inch square pan with shortening.

2 In medium bowl, stir together cookie mix, butter, peanut butter, vanilla and egg with spoon until soft dough forms (dough will be crumbly). Pat dough into pan.

3 Bake 18 to 22 minutes or until edges are dry and golden brown. Run knife around inside edge of pan. Place on cooling rack; cool about 1 hour.

4 Spread frosting over bars. For bars, cut into 4 rows by 4 rows.

1 Bar: Calories 280 (Calories from Fat 110); Total Fat 12g (Saturated Fat 5g; Trans Fat 1g); Cholesterol 25mg; Sodium 260mg; Total Carbohydrate 40g (Dietary Fiber 0g); Protein 3g **% Daily Value:** Vitamin A 2%; Vitamin C 0%; Calcium 4%; Iron 0% **Exchanges:** 1 Starch, 1½ Other Carbohydrate, 2½ Fat **Carbohydrate Choices:** 2½

No need to be square! Bake bars in an 8-inch or 9-inch round cake pan and frost as directed, cut into wedges to serve.

Cream Cheese–Swirl Brownies

Prep Time: 15 Minutes • Start to Finish: 2 Hours 30 Minutes • 16 brownies

FILLING

4 **oz (half of 8-oz package) cream cheese, softened**

3 **tablespoons sugar**

¼ **teaspoon pure vanilla**

1 **egg yolk**

BROWNIES

1 **box Betty Crocker® Gluten Free brownie mix**

¼ **cup butter, melted**

2 **whole eggs**

¼ **cup miniature semisweet chocolate chips**

1 Heat oven to 350°F (325°F for dark or nonstick pan). Spray bottom only of 9-inch square pan with cooking spray (without flour).

2 In small bowl, beat filling ingredients with electric mixer on low speed until smooth; set aside.

3 In medium bowl, stir brownie mix, butter and eggs until well blended (batter will be thick). Spread three-fourths of batter in pan. Spoon cream cheese filling by tablespoonfuls evenly onto brownie batter. Spoon remaining batter over filling. Cut through mixture with knife several times for marbled design. Sprinkle with chocolate chips.

4 Bake 37 to 44 minutes or until toothpick inserted 2 inches from side of pan comes out almost clean. Cool completely in pan on cooling rack, about 1 hour 30 minutes. Cut into 4 rows by 4 rows. Store covered in refrigerator.

1 Serving: Calories 210 (Calories from Fat 80); Total Fat 9g (Saturated Fat 5g; Trans Fat 0g); Cholesterol 55mg; Sodium 110mg; Total Carbohydrate 28g (Dietary Fiber 1g); Protein 2g **% Daily Value:** Vitamin A 4%; Vitamin C 0%; Calcium 0%; Iron 8% **Exchanges:** ½ Starch, 1½ Other Carbohydrate, 1½ Fat **Carbohydrate Choices:** 2

Use a small trigger ice cream scoop to easily spoon the cream cheese filling over the brownie batter and the reserved batter evenly over the filling.

Cappuccino Brownies

Prep Time: 15 Minutes • Start to Finish: 1 Hour 50 Minutes • 16 brownies

BROWNIES

- **2 teaspoons instant espresso coffee powder, coffee granules or crystals**
- **2 teaspoons water**
- **1 box Betty Crocker® Gluten Free brownie mix**
- **¼ cup butter, melted**
- **2 eggs**

FROSTING

- **2 teaspoons instant espresso coffee powder, coffee granules or crystals**
- **1 teaspoon water**
- **1 cup Betty Crocker® Rich & Creamy vanilla frosting (from 1-lb container)**
- **Chocolate-covered espresso beans or chocolate sprinkles, if desired**

1 Heat oven to 350°F (325°F for dark or nonstick pan). Spray bottom only of 8- or 9-inch square pan with cooking spray (without flour).

2 In medium bowl, stir 2 teaspoons espresso powder in 2 teaspoons water until dissolved. Stir in brownie mix, butter and eggs until well blended (batter will be thick). Spread in pan.

3 Bake 8-inch pan 28 to 31 minutes, 9-inch pan 26 to 30 minutes, or until toothpick inserted 2 inches from side of pan comes out almost clean. Cool in pan on cooling rack, about 1 hour.

4 In small bowl, stir 2 teaspoons espresso powder in 1 teaspoon water until dissolved. Stir in frosting until blended. Spread over brownies. Garnish with espresso beans or chocolate sprinkles.

1 Serving: Calories 220 (Calories from Fat 70); Total Fat 8g (Saturated Fat 3.5g; Trans Fat 1g); Cholesterol 35mg; Sodium 125mg; Total Carbohydrate 36g (Dietary Fiber 1g); Protein 2g **% Daily Value:** Vitamin A 2%; Vitamin C 0%; Calcium 0%; Iron 6% **Exchanges:** ½ Starch, 2 Other Carbohydrate, 1½ Fat **Carbohydrate Choices:** 2½

Add coffeehouse flavor to these brownies by sprinkling them with chopped toasted hazelnuts (filberts).

Enjoy even more mocha flavor by using chocolate frosting instead of vanilla.

German Chocolate Brownies

Prep Time: 15 Minutes • Start to Finish: 2 Hours • 16 brownies

BROWNIES

- 1 **box Betty Crocker® Gluten Free brownie mix**
- ¼ **cup butter, melted**
- 2 **eggs**
- ¼ **cup miniature semisweet chocolate chips**

COCONUT-PECAN FROSTING

- ⅓ **cup packed brown sugar**
- ⅓ **cup evaporated milk (from 5-oz can)**
- 1 **egg**
- ¼ **cup butter, cut into pieces**
- ¾ **cup flaked coconut**
- ⅓ **cup chopped pecans**
- ½ **teaspoon pure vanilla**

1 Heat oven to 350°F (325°F for dark or nonstick pan). Spray bottom only of 8- or 9-inch square pan with cooking spray (without flour).

2 In medium bowl, stir brownie mix, melted butter, 2 eggs and the chocolate chips until well blended (batter will be thick). Spread batter in pan.

3 Bake 8-inch pan 28 to 31 minutes, 9-inch pan 26 to 30 minutes, or until toothpick inserted 2 inches from side of pan comes out almost clean. Cool in pan on cooling rack.

4 Meanwhile, in 1-quart heavy saucepan, stir brown sugar, milk and 1 egg until well blended. Stir in cut-up butter. Cook over medium heat, stirring constantly, until mixture begins to bubble. Remove from heat. Stir in coconut, pecans and vanilla. Cool 15 minutes or until slightly thickened.

5 Frost brownies. Cool completely, about 1 hour. Cut into 4 rows by 4 rows. Store covered in refrigerator.

1 Serving: Calories 270 (Calories from Fat 120); Total Fat 14g (Saturated Fat 8g; Trans Fat 0g); Cholesterol 55mg; Sodium 120mg; Total Carbohydrate 32g (Dietary Fiber 2g); Protein 3g **% Daily Value:** Vitamin A 4%; Vitamin C 0%; Calcium 2%; Iron 8% **Exchanges:** 1 Starch, 1 Other Carbohydrate, 2½ Fat **Carbohydrate Choices:** 2

Store opened packages of coconut tightly sealed in the refrigerator up to 6 months.

Joy of Coconut Brownies

Prep Time: 15 Minutes • Start to Finish: 2 Hours 10 Minutes • 16 brownies

BROWNIES

- **1 box Betty Crocker® Gluten Free brownie mix**
- **¼ cup butter, melted**
- **2 eggs**
- **½ cup chopped almonds**

COCONUT TOPPING

- **1½ cups flaked coconut**
- **¾ cup sweetened condensed milk (not evaporated)**
- **16 whole almonds**

1 Heat oven to 350°F (325°F for dark or nonstick pan). Spray bottom only of 8- or 9-inch square pan with cooking spray (without flour).

2 In medium bowl, stir brownie mix, butter, eggs and chopped almonds until well blended (batter will be thick). Spread batter in pan. Bake 22 to 27 minutes or until top of brownies look moist but set.

3 In small bowl, mix coconut and condensed milk. Carefully spoon mixture evenly over hot brownies; spread evenly. Place whole almonds in 4 by 4 pattern on top so each brownie will have an almond in center when cut.

4 Bake 20 to 25 minutes longer or until topping is set and light golden brown. Cool completely in pan on cooling rack, about 1 hour. Cut into 4 rows by 4 rows.

1 Serving: Calories 290 (Calories from Fat 130); Total Fat 14g (Saturated Fat 8g; Trans Fat 0g); Cholesterol 40mg; Sodium 110mg; Total Carbohydrate 35g (Dietary Fiber 3g); Protein 4g **% Daily Value:** Vitamin A 4%; Vitamin C 0%; Calcium 6%; Iron 10% **Exchanges:** 1 Starch, 1½ Other Carbohydrate, 2½ Fat **Carbohydrate Choices:** 2

Not a nut lover? Omit the almonds and drizzle melted chocolate over baked brownies.

Peppermint Frosted Brownies

Prep Time: 15 Minutes • Start to Finish: 45 Minutes • 12 brownies

BROWNIES

- ⅓ **cup unsweetened baking cocoa**
- ¼ **cup white rice flour**
- ¼ **cup potato starch flour**
- ½ **teaspoon xanthan gum**
- ¼ **teaspoon gluten-free baking powder**
- ⅓ **cup sunflower or canola oil or melted ghee**
- ¾ **cup granulated sugar**
- 2 **eggs**
- 2 **teaspoons pure vanilla**

FROSTING

- ¼ **cup melted ghee or sunflower or canola oil**
- ½ **teaspoon pure vanilla**
- ¼ **teaspoon pure peppermint extract or oil**
- 1 **cup gluten-free powdered sugar**
- 2½ **teaspoons almond milk, soymilk or regular milk**
- 2 **tablespoons miniature semisweet chocolate chips**

1 Heat oven to 350°F. Line 8-inch square pan with foil, leaving 1 inch of foil overhanging at 2 opposite sides of pan; spray foil with cooking spray (without flour).

2 In small bowl, mix cocoa, flours, xanthan gum and baking powder; set aside. In medium bowl, beat oil, granulated sugar, eggs and 2 teaspoons vanilla with electric mixer on medium speed until well blended. Gradually add flour mixture, beating until well blended. Pour batter into pan.

3 Bake 25 minutes or until toothpick inserted in center comes out clean. Cool completely in pan on cooling rack.

4 In medium bowl, beat ghee, ½ teaspoon vanilla and the peppermint extract with electric mixer on medium speed. Gradually add powdered sugar and milk, beating until frosting is smooth and spreadable. If frosting is too thick, stir in additional milk, 1 teaspoon at a time. Stir in chocolate chips. Using foil, lift brownies out of pan; peel off foil. Frost brownies. Cut into 3 rows by 4 rows.

1 Brownie: Calories 240 (Calories from Fat 110); Total Fat 12g (Saturated Fat 4g; Trans Fat 0g); Cholesterol 45mg; Sodium 25mg; Total Carbohydrate 31g (Dietary Fiber 1g); Protein 1g **% Daily Value:** Vitamin A 4%; Vitamin C 0%; Calcium 0%; Iron 4% **Exchanges:** ½ Starch, 1½ Other Carbohydrate, 2½ Fat **Carbohydrate Choices:** 2

Contributed by Jean Duane Alternative Cook http://www.alternativecook.com

Peppermint oil is found in the spice aisle of most supermarkets and does not contain alcohol. Peppermint extract contains peppermint oil and alcohol. Either will work in this recipe.

Whoopie Pie Brownies

Prep Time: 20 Minutes • Start to Finish: 2 Hours 25 Minutes • 16 brownies

BROWNIES

- 1 box Betty Crocker® Gluten Free brownie mix
- ¼ cup butter, melted
- 2 eggs

TOPPING

- 1 cup gluten-free powdered sugar
- ½ cup butter or margarine, softened
- 1 cup marshmallow crème (from 7- or 13-oz jar)
- 1 teaspoon pure vanilla
- ¼ cup semisweet chocolate chips

1 Heat oven to 350°F (325°F for dark or nonstick pan). Spray bottom only of 8- or 9-inch square pan with cooking spray (without flour).

2 In medium bowl, stir brownie mix, ¼ cup butter and the eggs until well blended (batter will be thick). Spread batter in pan.

3 Bake 8-inch pan 28 to 31 minutes, 9-inch pan 26 to 30 minutes, or until toothpick inserted 2 inches from side of pan comes out almost clean. Cool completely in pan on cooling rack, about 1 hour.

4 In medium bowl, beat powdered sugar and ½ cup butter with electric mixer on medium speed until light and fluffy. Beat in marshmallow creme and vanilla on low speed until combined. Spread over brownies.

5 In small resealable freezer plastic bag, place chocolate chips; seal bag. Microwave on High 30 to 60 seconds, kneading bag every 15 seconds, until chocolate is melted and smooth. Cut tiny corner off bag; squeeze bag to drizzle chocolate over brownies. Let stand 30 minutes or until chocolate is set. Cut into 4 rows by 4 rows. Store loosely covered at room temperature.

1 Serving: Calories 270 (Calories from Fat 110); Total Fat 12g (Saturated Fat 7g; Trans Fat 0g); Cholesterol 50mg; Sodium 135mg; Total Carbohydrate 38g (Dietary Fiber 1g); Protein 2g **% Daily Value:** Vitamin A 6%; Vitamin C 0%; Calcium 0%; Iron 6% **Exchanges:** ½ Starch, 2 Other Carbohydrate, 2½ Fat **Carbohydrate Choices:** 2½

Whoopie pies originated in New England as mound-shaped chocolate cakes filled with a marshmallow-crème filling.

Zucchini Brownies with Fudge Frosting

Prep Time: 15 Minutes • Start to Finish: 2 Hours 25 Minutes • 16 brownies

BROWNIES

1 **box Betty Crocker® Gluten Free brownie mix**

¼ **cup butter, melted**

2 **eggs**

1 **cup shredded zucchini**

FROSTING

3 **tablespoons butter**

1½ **oz unsweetened baking chocolate**

1½ **cups gluten-free powdered sugar**

2 **to 3 tablespoons milk**

1 Heat oven to 350°F (325°F for dark or nonstick pan). Spray bottom only of 8- or 9-inch square pan with cooking spray (without flour).

2 In medium bowl, stir brownie mix, ¼ cup butter, the eggs and zucchini until well blended (batter will be thick). Spread batter in pan.

3 Bake 33 to 38 minutes or until toothpick inserted 2 inches from side of pan comes out almost clean. Cool completely in pan on cooling rack, about 1 hour 30 minutes.

4 In medium microwavable bowl, microwave 3 tablespoons butter and the chocolate uncovered on High about 1 minute, stirring once, until melted. Stir in powdered sugar and enough milk to make frosting smooth and spreadable. Frost brownies. Cut into 4 rows by 4 rows.

1 Serving: Calories 230 (Calories from Fat 80); Total Fat 8g (Saturated Fat 5g; Trans Fat 0g); Cholesterol 40mg; Sodium 105mg; Total Carbohydrate 36g (Dietary Fiber 1g); Protein 2g **% Daily Value:** Vitamin A 4%; Vitamin C 0%; Calcium 0%; Iron 8% **Exchanges:** ½ Starch, 2 Other Carbohydrate, 1½ Fat **Carbohydrate Choices:** 2½

The bake time for this recipe is longer than the box directions because there is additional moisture in the brownies from the zucchini.

For smooth and shiny frosting, dip metal spatula in hot water and wipe dry. Slide heated knife over frosting; repeat if needed.

Black Forest Brownie Squares

Prep Time: 20 Minutes • Start to Finish: 1 Hour 20 Minutes • 12 servings

BROWNIES

1 box Betty Crocker® Gluten Free brownie mix

¼ cup butter, melted

2 eggs

1 tablespoon cherry liqueur, if desired

CHERRY FILLING

1 can (15 oz) pitted dark sweet cherries in heavy syrup, drained, ¼ cup syrup reserved

2 tablespoons cornstarch

1 tablespoon cherry liqueur or water

SWEETENED WHIPPED CREAM

1 cup whipping cream

2 tablespoons gluten-free powdered sugar

TOPPING

½ oz semisweet baking chocolate, shaved

1 Heat oven to 350°F (325°F for dark or nonstick pan). Spray bottom only of 8- or 9-inch square pan with cooking spray (without flour).

2 In medium bowl, stir brownie mix, butter, eggs and 1 tablespoon liqueur until well blended (batter will be thick). Spread batter in pan.

3 Bake 8-inch pan 28 to 31 minutes, 9-inch pan 26 to 30 minutes, or until toothpick inserted 2 inches from side of pan comes out almost clean. Cool completely in pan on cooling rack, about 1 hour.

4 Meanwhile, in 2-quart heavy saucepan, stir reserved syrup and the cornstarch until combined. Stir in cherries. Cook over medium heat, stirring constantly, until thickened (cherries will break down and mixture will be very thick). Remove from heat; stir in 1 tablespoon liqueur. Cool at least 30 minutes. Spread filling evenly over brownies.

5 In chilled medium bowl, beat whipping cream and powdered sugar with electric mixer on low speed until mixture begins to thicken. Gradually increase speed to high, beating just until soft peaks form. Spread whipped cream over filling; sprinkle with chocolate shavings. Serve or refrigerate. Cut into 4 rows by 3 rows. Store covered in refrigerator.

1 Serving: Calories 320 (Calories from Fat 130); Total Fat 14g (Saturated Fat 8g; Trans Fat 0g); Cholesterol 70mg; Sodium 125mg; Total Carbohydrate 44g (Dietary Fiber 2g); Protein 3g **% Daily Value:** Vitamin A 8%; Vitamin C 0%; Calcium 2%; Iron 10% **Exchanges:** 1 Starch, 2 Other Carbohydrate, 2½ Fat **Carbohydrate Choices:** 3

Substitute 1 can (21 oz) cherry pie filling for the cooked filling, but check the ingredients first to make sure all are gluten-free.

For foolproof whipped cream, freeze the bowl and beaters at least 10 minutes before whipping the cream.

Mexican Chocolate Brownies

Prep Time: 15 Minutes • Start to Finish: 2 Hours 15 Minutes • 16 brownies

3 cups Cinnamon Chex® cereal

3 tablespoons packed brown sugar

¼ teaspoon baking soda

½ cup butter or margarine, melted

1 box Betty Crocker® Gluten Free brownie mix

2 eggs

1 Heat oven to 350°F. Spray bottom only of 8-inch square pan with cooking spray (without flour). Place cereal in resealable food-storage plastic bag; seal bag and crush with rolling pin to make about 1½ cups.

2 In medium bowl, mix crushed cereal, brown sugar and baking soda; stir in ¼ cup melted butter until well mixed. Reserve ⅓ cup cereal mixture for topping. Press remaining cereal mixture evenly in bottom of pan. Bake 5 minutes. Cool 5 minutes.

3 Meanwhile, in medium bowl, stir brownie mix, ¼ cup melted butter and the eggs until well blended. Drop batter by small spoonfuls over baked layer. Carefully spread over baked layer; sprinkle with reserved ⅓ cup cereal mixture.

4 Bake 30 to 34 minutes or until brownies look dry and set. (Brownies will be soft; do not use toothpick test.) Cool completely, about 1 hour 30 minutes. For brownies, cut into 4 rows by 4 rows. Store tightly covered.

1 Brownie: Calories 190 (Calories from Fat 50); Total Fat 6g (Saturated Fat 3g; Trans Fat 0g); Cholesterol 35mg; Sodium 150mg; Total Carbohydrate 33g (Dietary Fiber 0g); Protein 2g **% Daily Value:** Vitamin A 6%; Vitamin C 0%; Calcium 4%; Iron 25% **Exchanges:** 1 Starch, 1 Other Carbohydrate, 1 Fat **Carbohydrate Choices:** 2

Always read labels to make sure each recipe ingredient is gluten-free. Products and ingredient sources can change.

Safe to Consume Gluten-Free Ingredients

The following ingredients are safe to consume, if you are following a gluten-free lifestyle:

- Acorn
- Almond
- Amaranth
- Arborio rice
- Aromatic rice
- Arrowroot
- Basmati rice
- Brown rice, brown rice flour
- Buckwheat
- Calrose
- Canola
- Cassava
- Channa
- Chestnut
- Chickpea (Garbanzo)
- Corn, corn flour, corn gluten, corn malt, cornmeal, cornstarch
- Cottonseed
- Dal
- Dasheen flour
- Enriched rice
- Fava bean
- Flax, flaxseed
- Garbanzo
- Glutinous rice
- Hominy
- Instant rice
- Job's tears
- Millet
- Modified cornstarch
- Modified tapioca starch
- Montina™
- Peanut flour
- Potato flour, potato starch flour
- Quinoa
- Red rice
- Rice, rice bran, rice flour
- Risotto
- Sago
- Sesame, sesame seed
- Sorghum
- Soy, soybean, tofu (soya)
- Starch (made from safe grains)
- Sunflower seed
- Sweet rice flour
- Tapioca
- Taro flour
- Teff
- Wild rice

Safe to Consume Gluten-Free Additives

The following additives are safe to consume, if you are following a gluten-free lifestyle:

- Acacia gum (gum arabic)
- Adipic acid
- Algin
- Annatto
- Aspartame
- Baking yeast
- Benzoic acid
- Beta carotene
- BHA
- BHT
- Brewer's yeast
- Brown sugar
- Calcium disodium EDTA
- Carrageenan
- Caramel color[1]
- Carboxymethyl cellulose
- Carob bean gum
- Cellulose
- Corn syrup
- Corn syrup solids
- Cream of tartar
- Dextrose
- Ethyl maltol
- Fructose
- Fumaric acid
- Gelatin
- Glucose
- Guar gum
- Invert sugar
- Karaya gum
- Lactic acid
- Lactose
- Lecithin
- Malic acid
- Maltodextrin[2]
- Maltol
- Mannitol
- Methylcellulose
- MSG (monosodium glutamate)
- Papain
- Pectin
- Polysorbate 60; 80
- Propylene glycol
- Psyllium
- Sodium benzoate
- Sodium metabisulfite
- Sodium nitrate; nitrite
- Sodium sulfite
- Sorbitol
- Stearic acid
- Sucralose
- Sucrose
- Sugar
- Tartaric acid
- Tartrazine
- Titanium dioxide
- Tragacanth
- Vanilla extract
- Vanillan
- White vinegar[3]
- Xanthan gum
- Xylitol
- Yam
- Yeast

1 Caramel color is manufactured by heating carbohydrates and is produced from sweeteners. Although gluten-containing ingredients can be used, they are not used in North America; corn is most often used; however, it is important to check with food manufacturers.

2 Maltodextrin is made from cornstarch, potato starch or rice starch.

3 Distilled white vinegar is safe to consume on the gluten-free diet. Vinegar is a solution made of acetic acid and flavoring materials such as apples, grapes, grain and molasses. For example, cider vinegar is made from apple juice; malt vinegar is made from barley malt; balsamic vinegar is made from grapes. Distilled vinegars are gluten-free because the distillation process filters out the large gluten proteins so that they do not pass through to the end product. Therefore, the finished liquid is gluten free. Patients with celiac disease should not be concerned about distilled white vinegar or foods such as pickles, which may contain it. The exception to this rule is MALT VINEGAR, which is not distilled, and therefore is not safe to consume.

For More Information

University of Chicago Celiac Disease Center   http://www.celiacdisease.net/
University of Maryland Center for Celiac Research   http://celiaccenter.org/
Visit www.glutenfreely.com
Celiac Sprue Association   http://www.csaceliacs.info
Celiac Disease Foundation   http://www.celiac.org/
Bell Institute of Health and Nutrition   http://www.bellinstitute.com/
Gluten Free Dining Out Toolbox by K. Koeller and R. La France

Metric Conversion Guide

Volume

U.S. UNITS	CANADIAN METRIC	AUSTRALIAN METRIC
¼ teaspoon	1 mL	1 ml
½ teaspoon	2 mL	2 ml
1 teaspoon	5 mL	5 ml
1 tablespoon	15 mL	20 ml
¼ cup	50 mL	60 ml
⅓ cup	75 mL	80 ml
½ cup	125 mL	125 ml
⅔ cup	150 mL	170 ml
¾ cup	175 mL	190 ml
1 cup	250 mL	250 ml
1 quart	1 liter	1 liter
1½ quarts	1.5 liters	1.5 liters
2 quarts	2 liters	2 liters
2½ quarts	2.5 liters	2.5 liters
3 quarts	3 liters	3 liters
4 quarts	4 liters	4 liters

Measurements

INCHES	CENTIMETERS
1	2.5
2	5.0
3	7.5
4	10.0
5	12.5
6	15.0
7	17.5
8	20.5
9	23.0
10	25.5
11	28.0
12	30.5
13	33.0

Weight

U.S. UNITS	CANADIAN METRIC	AUSTRALIAN METRIC
1 ounce	30 grams	30 grams
2 ounces	55 grams	60 grams
3 ounces	85 grams	90 grams
4 ounces (¼ pound)	115 grams	125 grams
8 ounces (½ pound)	225 grams	225 grams
16 ounces (1 pound)	455 grams	500 grams
1 pound	455 grams	0.5 kilogram

Temperatures

FAHRENHEIT	CELSIUS
32°	0°
212°	100°
250°	120°
275°	140°
300°	150°
325°	160°
350°	180°
375°	190°
400°	200°
425°	220°
450°	230°
475°	240°
500°	260°

NOTE: The recipes in this cookbook have not been developed or tested using metric measures. When converting recipes to metric, some variations in quality may be noted.

Index

Page numbers in *italics* indicate illustrations.